THE ONLINE WORLD

WHAT YOU THINK YOU KNOW AND WHAT YOU DON'T

4 CRITICAL TOOLS FOR
RAISING KIDS IN THE DIGITAL AGE

RANIA MANKARIOUS, MA, JD
CEO OF CRIME STOPPERS OF HOUSTON

SILVERSMITH
PRESS

Copyright © 2021, 2022 Rania Mankarious

All rights reserved. No portion of this book may be reproduced in any form or by any means—electronic, mechanical, photocopy, recording, scanning, or other—except for brief quotations in critical reviews or articles, without the prior written permission of the author.

Published in Houston, Texas, by Silversmith Press.

Silversmith Press titles may be purchased in bulk for educational, business, fundraising, or sales promotional use. For information please email, office@silversmithpress.com.

Any internet addresses, phone numbers, or company or product information printed in this book are offered as a resource and are not intended in any way to be or to imply an endorsement by the author and/or Silversmith Press, nor does the author and/or Silversmith Press vouch for the existence, content, or services of these sites, phone numbers, companies, or products beyond the life of this book.

ISBN 978-1-7378859-3-1 (Hardcover)
ISBN 978-1-7378859-2-4 (Softcover)
ISBN 978-1-7378859-1-7 (eBook)

Published by Silversmith Press, Houston, Texas—www.silversmithpress.com.
Printed in the United States of America.

*To my parents, Onsy and Suzie,
who fought heaven and earth to give me
and my sister every opportunity.*

*To my sister, Nash, who always has been and
always will be my biggest role model.*

*To my husband, Ramy, who is my
backbone, protector and love of my life.*

*And most importantly to my girls,
Olivia, Emma and Evelyn.
It's for you and because of you that I do absolutely everything. I love you more than life itself.*

CONTENTS

Appreciation 7

Foreword 11

Introduction 17

Section One—Online Foundations 27

Chapter 1 - The Good Kid 29

Chapter 2 - Your Child's Developing Inner World 53

Chapter 3 - Welcome to the Online Jungle 69

Chapter 4 - It's Time We Had a Talk 83

Chapter 5 - Apps, Challenges, and Chain Letters...Oh My! 91

Section Two—The Four Power Tools 119

Chapter 6 - Tool 1: Define Your Brand 121

Chapter 7 - Tool 2: Define Your Community 153

Chapter 8 - Tool 3: Develop an Exit Strategy 175

Chapter 9 - Internal Threats 227

Chapter 10 - Tool 4: Post Like a Celebrity 259

Chapter 11 - Resources for Parents 279

Index 312

APPRECIATION

Over the course of my professional life thus far, I've had one consistent wish—to put concepts I've developed into a book thereby creating an evergreen resource for parents to help keep kids safe online.

I carried this longing for years, unable to move forward until one day a dear friend, Gabriela Gerhart, introduced me to writing coach, Joanna Hunt-Boyer. In less than a year, Joanna helped me turn concepts into a plan, stories into action steps, and endless hours of research into the book you now hold in your hand. In the end, she has made a very real and personal dream come true, one that would not have happened without her.

A special thanks to Joanna for her writing expertise and to Chris Boyer for his creative direction, the amazing cover and interior design, and the team at Silversmith Press who brought this project to life.

Thank you to my daughter Olivia, for being a test reader and junior editor; Mary Maikhail, for offering honest parent feedback, and Alex Soliman for adding a college student's perspective!

Through it all, there were many 5:00 a.m. mornings, late nights, and busy weekends. My husband and children bore the brunt of the endless hours I poured into this effort. Their love, support, encouragement, coffee runs, snacks, neck massages and more kept me going, and my love for them made me as determined as ever to finish this work.

My parents and sister have been involved every step of the way, listening to ideas, concepts and helping on final title and design. I thank them for all they've done to shape my interest and get me to this point.

To my other family—the team at Crime Stoppers of Houston and my Houston community—you allow me to do work that means everything to me and to be a part of your lives during your most critical moments. You inspire me daily and give me hope for a better tomorrow.

To Dr. Laura Berman and Sam Chapman and all those who endorsed this book, thank you for using your powerful voices to further this work.

To parents reading this book—I thank you for advocating for your child and hope you find this resource helpful and hopeful. As I always say—I love my kids and I love yours too. I will never stop fighting for them.

—Rania

FOREWORD BY
DR. LAURA BERMAN & SAM CHAPMAN

In a perfect world, we never would have been asked to write this foreword. Not because we don't adore Rania and support her incredible mission, but because in our perfect world, Sammy is still here. Sammy, our forever 16-year-old, who was taken from this world thanks to SnapChat and online drug dealers. If Sammy was still here, we wouldn't know about how truly dangerous social media can be for kids. We wouldn't know about the insidious power of Big Social Media and the ways in which they skirt the law and avoid taking responsibility for the deaths that occur as a result of their platforms. We wouldn't know about the thousands of kids who have died as a result of online drug deals, cyberbullying, TikTok challenges, sexual predators and human trafficking.

If Sammy was here, up in his room tuning his guitar or laughing with his little brother as they play video games, we would still be blind and ignorant to the grave dangers of social media.

But he's not. He's gone forever, and the person responsible will never be held accountable, because social media protects and enables the worst kinds of criminals. So, here we are, writing a foreword we never could have imagined, writing a foreword pleading with other parents to join our fight and realize that every single child is at risk right now. Our boy was an A+ student. He was on the school football team. He was intelligent and ambitious, and so excited to start his summer internship. And now, his potential and purpose here has been snuffed out. All we can do is gather our grief and pain and use it to help educate other parents who may not be aware of how dangerous the online world is.

Like most parents, we supposed that the worst thing that could happen online would be that our sons might see a photo of a naked woman or be exposed to foul language. We had no idea this whole "other world" existed – one filled with drug dealers and pimps, predators and abusers. Until one day, we learned; and we learned in the worst possible way anyone could imagine.

You'll read our story in this book, and while there is nothing we can do to change the past, there is something we can do so that our story and our loss does not become your story or your loss. We are committed to sounding the alarm and making sure all parents wake up.

If you know our family, you know that we are active with full plates and full lives. We didn't choose this new trajectory, but we have embraced it with a fierce passion. Now, we are dedicated and committed to a conversation that exposes the unimaginable realities the dark web (or the everyday web) has on our children. We are dedicated to using our voices and our platforms to get the attention of every parent, who like us just a few months ago, doesn't fully comprehend the dangers of the online world. And most of all, beyond sounding the alarm, we are dedicated to providing answers. While many want kids to stay offline—and we do too—we realize that to some degree, that is not realistic in the digital age. We'd rather demand solutions and strategies that ensure the safety of all. Solutions that include demanding improved safety measures when it comes to big tech; solutions that no longer shield big tech from all liability; solutions that prohibit dangerous individuals from easily and swiftly fading in and out of children's messaging apps, offering our kids things that can alter their lives or end them. We're working with companies like BARK.us and on campaigns like #letparentsprotect as well as legislation (Sammy's Law) and we will not stop.

If you are a parent grieving a similar loss, please know that you are not alone. It is not your fault. And you have every right to honor your grief and feel your deep pain. Everyday we are learning anew how to dance with our grief and bend to its tides, rather than run from it. We know that the closer we hold Sammy in our hearts and the more we tell his story, the more we keep his legacy alive and help heal the world. And we are making progress; Facebook is finally facing legislative heat thanks to whistle-blowers who have called out the company's history of negating risks to young users, and we are hoping to see the power of Big Social Media be curtailed in the coming years.

For now, the fight continues. Please read on to learn how YOU can join this fight by helping to keep your kids and your loved ones safe online. A lot of care went into this book and into providing strategies and solutions that you can implement right now in your own homes. Take the time to go through this with your child. We promise you will never regret it.

—Dr. Laura Berman & Sam Chapman

INTRODUCTION

I am child of the 80s—a much simpler time with very little digital distractions. Atari, which launched in 1977, was the main gaming platform, but it only had a handful of games. I was an observant little girl. I was taught to be aware of my surroundings, my family, and our community. I was also aware that, while I was born in a town just 18 miles west of Boston, we were very much an immigrant family. My parents socialized with friends and relatives from their native country, and weekends were always booked with events with these community friends. I was aware that I looked slightly different from the other kids around me, with my curly dark hair and tan skin. I recognized that the parents at school had camaraderie that my family was not a part of. I noticed that my jam-packed lunches (and my mother really jam-packed them) were very different from my peers'.

Not only was I very aware that we were not native Bostonians, but I was also aware that my parents left our native country because we were minorities there too. Good or bad, we seemed to be "minorities" wherever we went.

While I was always conscious of it, it never bothered me and I only share it with you now as a backdrop for who I am, how I was raised, and ultimately how I came to write this book. In our home growing up, conversations were interesting and intentional. They were always filled with history, politics, current events, an assessment of present risks and dangers, as well as whatever was trending in society, positively or negatively. I remember when Christa McAuliffe, one of the seven crew members in the Space Shuttle Challenger disaster, was killed going to space. I was a kid of the Cold War. I remember when the Berlin Wall came down in the late 80s. I know many reading this book remember exactly where they were when 9/11 happened—and we remember it like yesterday. My generation navigated the birth of AOL, MySpace, and literally the internet itself. I actually remember life before cell phones—or cordless phones for that matter. My generation has seen a lot, and through it all, my parents, while culturally very tied to their community, raised me to actively think about the ramifications of all these things—to question everything. They also instilled in me the sense to work hard and invest in our city and community. "What will you do? How will you participate? What will it mean?" were a few questions they'd always ask.

I'll never forget late-night dinners in our 70s-style Boston home while the smoke from my father's cigarettes puffed about, not even an issue at the time. Those discussions around history, politics, current events, our continual assessments on present risks, dangers and the trending positives and negatives in society evolved through the 80s, 90s and early 2000s. They provided my life's backdrop as I navigated high school. They stayed with me through college, graduate school, my internships, and law school. I pondered them as I traveled between Boston and New York, working with people from all over the world, in my marketing and management position for a high-end fashion magazine. And it's because of these poignant conversations that I ended up working where I work now, as the CEO of Crime Stoppers of Houston.

While I was always clear about my interests and had a broad view of the world, I never wanted to live anywhere but the East Coast, and I certainly never wanted to work in the dark and often scary world of "crime." But life has a funny way of working out. I was being courted by a Texan doing his residency in Boston. (Yes, "courted by." Culturally that's how it is described.) We were headed towards marriage but the idea of moving to Texas gave me cold feet so I broke up with him. But since I loved him more than Boston, the breakup was short lived, and now I eat Tex-Mex say things like "y'all" without thinking. However, when I first arrived in Houston and read about the opening at Crime Stoppers, I wasn't initially going to apply. The website was terrible, and the name was lackluster. But, since I was new to the area and eager to get involved in the community somehow, I did anyway. Crime Stoppers was looking for an "attorney with a background in marketing" and that's what I was, so I applied for the position, more interested in the exercise of interviewing in this new and foreign "Texas" culture than anything else. Never would I have imagined that I would walk away from the interview so excited. (Side note: The position was actually for an internship that paid $10 an hour.) I'm sure it looked crazy from the outside for this attorney, with a master's degree in marriage and family therapy, and strong work experience from Boston and New York, to agree to work as an intern, the lowest rung on the vocation ladder, even at such an incredible Houston nonprofit. Many years later, I'm now honored to run this organization, doing work I find vital and fulfilling, alongside people I respect and admire so much. I remain deeply proud to serve the people of this great city, state, and beyond.

When I consider the valuable family conversations of my upbringing, I find it so disheartening that in the day we now live in, family discussions often take a back seat to devices and swiping through social platforms. These thought-provoking, insightful, and meaningful family conversations are few and far between, if they are taking place at all. Children today are often left to figure things out on their own, pulling life guidance from celebrities, influencers, and trending TikTok videos they are following online. But in all the change that's taken place through the years, there's something that hasn't. You can place 100 people in a room and find that they have 100 different stories, different interests, speak different languages, and have different outlooks on life. Still, of those 100 people, absolutely 100% will agree that the health and safety of themselves and their loved ones are amongst their top two greatest concerns. I have found that the lack of health and safety powerfully, equally, and universally brings us to our knees. I think of a terrifying cancer diagnosis, an addiction that steals the life of a young person, a mother robbed as her children watch helplessly, or the young woman who is relentlessly stalked or harassed. These issues level the playing field, unite us all, and for me spark great interest.

Never have all my life lessons and observations intersected in real time with universal events as powerfully as they did in 2020. I think we can all agree that 2020 had a tremendous impact on every facet of our society, from the Global Pandemic of Covid, to the death of George Floyd, to the defund police movement, to the push to have all children only connect virtually. I can say without exaggeration that health and safety are not only top priorities globally, but they are – now more than ever – directly affected by history, politics, current events, and directly tied to present risks, dangers, and what's trending good and bad in society.

As a lifelong observer of these realities, I continually follow the causes and consequences of all that is happening around us, looking specifically at the nexus between "life and safety" and offering solutions in the areas that present the most harm, specifically to children and families. Like a child who squeezes her eyes shut in bed at night with the hopes that the "boogie monster" won't get her, I often watch as parents do the same thing. They close their eyes to the reality of what's going on around them, pretending it will remove them or their children from the potential harm. I know this because I'm often one of the first people called when the harsh reality hits and parents are shocked at what has happened right under their noses. I work hard daily to protect children and families, whether acting in my role at Crime Stoppers or as a concerned and involved mother. I work with parents to reveal harmful false narratives, which we discuss later in this book, and explain the dangers of what can and does happen online. I focus on actual solutions parents can implement, that children can understand, agree with, and follow.

My whole mission, and that of the organization I work for, is keeping you and your children, your schools and your homes, your business, your retailers, parks, neighborhoods and more, safe–proactively. We serve every man, woman, child, and animal in our area and ultimately in yours. In my leadership role, I talk to people all the time about their concerns. I am constantly listening, reading, and researching. I've written over 200 published articles on public safety and have done countless media interviews on all aspects of family safety. I examine the myths of safety, the realities of crime, and how they interface with current trends and sadly, the growing depravity of society. I am shocked by what I see now and where we are headed. So many people build walls subconsciously to either keep the danger at bay or to convince themselves the dangers aren't in their lives or affecting their kids–but that's not reality.

The premise for this book comes from being "in the field" and having boots-on-the-ground conversations with children and parents who can, at times, seem worlds apart on such important, and potentially dangerous issues. I've encountered parents who think their children are safe online because they "live in a good neighborhood" or send their kids to the "best private schools." Other parents tell me they know their kids are safe online because "they've been raised right." And still there are others who choose to deal with everything by forcing social restrictions on their children, such as forbidding them from having any online or social media engagement with their peers. I don't recommend this for several reasons. First, it's a form of social punishment that is unfair for your child. Second, nine times out of ten, your child will absolutely and without question still have online accounts without you knowing about it. (Yes, even *your* child is capable of this.) This means they are navigating these extremely dangerous and toxic platforms completely on their own, with no guidance or instruction from anyone other than their peers and the complete strangers on these platforms with them. Yes, even if they are great kids and have terrific friends, go to a good school, and seemingly never disobey you, when it comes to the online world, the reality is...all bets are off.

In this book, we are going to take the topic of the online world head on. Trust me, this book has been years in the making. Not surprisingly, most books, articles, studies, and published papers explain why our kids should not be online, or gaming, because the risks and dangers are so powerfully overwhelming. I've read it all, and by the way, I agree. But I also know, having talked to today's kids and considering the reality of the world we live in, we will not succeed in keeping kids offline. We just won't. And so we have to prepare them and ourselves. Together, we need to find a way to rise above the tidal wave of platforms, apps, and constantly changing technology to give our kids the tools to stay safe and healthy while broaching these dangerous waters. Here's the deal—I love my kids and I love yours too. I love all kids and I want to keep them safe. Each day, I wake up thankful for the wonders of technology, while at the same time, I try to balance the very significant issues that technology creates for the children we love, who are simply trying to make their way to adulthood.

This book will equip families to engage in relevant conversations to help kids safely navigate the online world in all its forms and address social media, cyber safety and security, gaming, digital streaming, and more. The core of this book is my four-tool strategy to help shape your child's perspective and approach to the way they engage in online environments. In the end, you'll no longer need to play "catch up" with the online world while your child bolts seamlessly past you. Instead, you will have the tools in place and the groundwork laid to protect them proactively and over the long run, regardless of where they go online. In a world where we must be honest and fair and recognize the wonderful value of the digital world, we must still, with blinders off and fueled with fierce determination, do everything we can to protect our children.

HOW TO READ THIS BOOK

Over the years that I have envisioned this book, I constantly said to myself and to my publisher, "I want this to be like the book *What to Expect When You're Expecting* but in the realm of the online world." That may sound strange to some, but I wanted it to be a timeless resource for parents to go back to, time and time again. Something they could read from start to finish, or skim through to find what was relevant in the moment, or simply search topically. Having said that, I want to give you permission to use this book any way you see fit, as your reference guide for raising kids in the digital age.

I also want to warn you: There is a lot of information in here, so buckle up! Throughout this book, you will find startling facts and statistics, resources, exercises, and questions to discuss with your teen/tween/kid as they face the reality of the online world. I strongly recommend that you read this entire book yourself first and highlight or mark what stands out to you. Then, make sure your coparent or any authority figure in your child's life has a copy as well so you can all be on the same page, or at least coming from the same place of understanding. After you've read through the book, go back through it with your child and complete the exercises and questions. In Chapter 11, there's a step-by-step action guide to walk you through each exercise so you can build a smart online plan that works for you and your family.

SECTION ONE

ONLINE FOUNDATIONS

CHAPTER 1

The Good Kid

No parent ever wants to think their child is at risk of death, but the truth is, if your child is on a device, they are at risk for a lot of things.

"My heart is completely shattered and I'm not sure how to keep breathing. I post this now only so that not one more kid dies."

Sammy's mother sat hunched on the sofa. Her 16-year-old's motionless body lay upstairs on his bedroom floor in their suburban California home where they had been sheltering in place due to Covid-19. She could barely get the words typed into her social post on her phone as she sobbed uncontrollably, gasping for air. Every fiber of her being was engulfed in the most excruciating grief. A glowing mother of three thriving boys, now a grieving mother of two, forced down a new path in life. That day changed their family forever. Social media changed their family forever.

How could this be happening?
I wasn't gone long. He didn't want to die. He was a straight A student with goals and dreams.
He was happy, well liked, smart, funny, and kind.

CHAPTER ONE

He had a great family with two very involved parents.
He was a good kid.

Up until that moment, it had been a regular day in the Chapman household; it was a happy day. Laura, her husband Sam, and two of their three sons, Sammy and Jackson, were getting ready to watch Super Bowl LV that Sunday evening. The state of California had been under lockdown orders due to Covid-19 but Laura was determined to make the most of the time. As an internationally acclaimed expert in the field of sex and relationship therapy, a New York Times bestselling author, award-winning radio host, podcast host, and TV personality known for her regular appearances on Today, Good Morning America, and the OWN Network, where she previously hosted her own show, Dr. Laura Berman welcomed the opportunity for extra connection time with her family. She had some errands to run that day with her youngest son, Jackson, but before leaving, her middle son, Sammy, said, "Hey Mom! When you get back, I want to talk to you about an internship I'd like to apply for." Laura smiled. "Sure son. We can talk when I get back."

Sammy was a straight-A student; always looking for opportunities and planning for his future. Laura and Sam were proud of him, as they are of all their children. Laura ran her errands, which always took longer than planned because even with a mask, there was always someone who recognized her or stopped to chat for a minute or two. Upon arriving back home, she pulled into the driveway and carried her things into the house. Jackson ran upstairs just ahead of her, wanting to see what Sammy was doing. He pushed the door open and shouted in horror. Jackson ran out of his brother's room shouting, "Sammy's on the floor!" Laura entered his room to find Sammy on his back unconscious, having aspirated on his own vomit. She shouted to her husband, who came running and immediately started CPR while Laura frantically called 911. It was terrifying and shocking—every parent's worst nightmare.

The paramedics arrived and tried for 30 minutes to resuscitate him to no avail. It was too late. What they would learn in the minutes, hours, and days to come sends chills down my spine. Once again, SnapChat outsmarted another family. Without his parents ever knowing it, social media allowed Sammy to easily and directly connect with a drug dealer and pill pusher. Without Sammy ever knowing it, what he thought he'd purchased was not at all what he ended up getting. With a click here and a click there, Sammy ordered one pill (presumably Percocet or Xanax) and had it delivered directly to the Chapman house (or very close by) for a fee of only 15 cents. On February 7, 2021, at the age of 16, that one 15-cent pill killed Sammy almost immediately after ingesting it.

The truth is, laced with Fentanyl, Sammy—a non-drug user, a good kid—didn't stand a chance. And his parents, good parents, involved parents, committed parents, were parents who, like so many of us, were unaware of the grave yet very

CHAPTER ONE

real dangers of the online world.

As the Chapmans dove in to learn more, they made another discovery. Law enforcement couldn't access Sammy's phone as the phone company would not release Sammy's personal information. The SnapChat messages had already disappeared; however, one of Sammy's friends had a screen shot from Sammy. It was the menu of pills this online pill pusher was selling. SnapChat won't release the identity of the account holder who delivered the drugs–to protect the pill pusher's privacy. They will only shut the account down, but sadly, that dealer will be up again with a new account name, pushing more drugs and pills on a colorful menu to an unimaginable number of kids.

Sammy's story is not isolated. Every day, children and teens are contacted by pill pushers and drug dealers who pretend to be selling familiar pills like Tylenol, Adderall, Percocet, or Xanax to kids who might want to take them for a whole host of reasons, none one of which is to "get high." Adolescents thrive on curiosity, and they are wired to push boundaries. They give no thought to where the drugs come from or if they were manufactured out of the country or locally in someone's garage. They don't understand that no one is regulating what's going in them and, shockingly and horrifically, Fentanyl is finding its way into an overwhelming number of street pills. Kids don't understand that drug dealers use Fentanyl in droves because it's highly addictive and cheap to get. Their goal is to get a young user hooked on a 15-cent pill. Once hooked, they will do what it takes to get more, regardless of the price. The dealers make delivery as easy as possible. Thanks to the GPS tracking that most online apps provide, a dealer can deliver the drugs to a child's front door without anyone else ever knowing. Sadly, hundreds and hundreds of kids die in the process, but the dealers, of course, do not care.

Laura and Sam never imagined that their son was at risk of doing anything that would put him in harm's way. They had boundaries set in place for his social media use and monitored his friends. He was a good kid with goals and dreams. He was at home in his room. "The last thing you think when your child is upstairs talking to his friends on SnapChat is that he's going to find a drug dealer who will deliver drugs to your house," Laura said.

Today, the Chapmans are leading voices in the fight to protect children online. They've learned about Narcan nasal spray, which is an over-the-counter medication that mitigates symptoms of opioid overdose, and they urge every home in America to have it on hand. They're working on their petition #LetParentsProtect and are advocating for parent monitoring services like BARK.us to be allowed on all platforms. They're advocating for legislative changes and opening the door for critical conversations.

No parent ever wants to think their child is at risk of death, but the truth is, if your child is on a device, they are at risk for a lot of things. And let's be honest, even if you haven't given your child a device, they will likely have access to one from somewhere; school, friends, etc. Your kids are at risk. My kids are at risk. Simply put, all kids are at risk. What this book will do is open the door for conversations toward awareness, learning, and growing, so you can turn the intangible, gray space of the online world into an understood and defined territory with boundaries. Once the unknown becomes known, you can place important, evergreen guardrails around your kid that really could save their lives.

LET'S PAINT A PICTURE

Preparing your kids for the online world is crucial. Kids have no idea what they are getting into when they go online, and most parents don't either.

But let's take a look at some numbers:

- The majority of our kids are accessing the online world either from home or school, at least 77% of kids ages 11–14 and 85% of kids ages 15–18 (these are pre-Covid numbers). Sadly, not only are a majority of kids accessing the online world, of those, approximately 90% will also be exposed to pornography as early as eight years old.[1]

- Beyond online access and viewing pornography, another 77% of young adults 15–25 years old shared that they

---

1 Data according to the National Center for Education Statistics www.guardchild.com

already use social media regularly to purchase drugs.[2]

- **And here's a sobering reality:** A majority of parents (72% in a pre-Covid study) shared that, honestly, they have no idea what their children are doing online.[3] This means only one thing—millions of children and young teens are navigating the wild, wild, west of the online world, a world in which they are outsmarted daily, with virtually no parental guidance. Parents, we must step in and close the gap!

Even though experts agree, myself included, that social media, gaming, and online engagement have many detrimental consequences, we also know that no matter what experts or parents say, our kids will still be online. Covid has forced this, society forces it, social norms expect it, and the chances that today's tweens or teens will turn their backs on all of this because "the experts say so" are slim to none. Mind you, I wish we could all work together to collectively encourage every teen to delete SnapChat, TikTok, Instagram, OnlyFans, or Omegle. I also wish we could demand that these platforms make the safety of our kids their number one priority[4] and that legislation would be written from the same perspective, with significant consequences when children

---

2 https://journals.copmadrid.org/ejpalc/art/ejpalc2021a5
3 https://www.prnewswire.com/il/news-releases/jiminy-72-of-parents-have-no-idea-what-their-children-are-doing-online-300789940.html
4 As I write this, a whistleblower has come forward alleging Facebook and Instagram have conducted internal studies that highlight the negative impact their platforms have on youth. She further states that those studies are ignored, and proper adjustments are not being made to the platforms because that would impact the company's financial bottom line.

CHAPTER ONE

are exploited, targeted, and killed because of their online engagement. But as of the time of this writing, that's not the case. It's up to us, parents, to come together and demand it. So back to our current reality. Our kids are online and they are not safe there. If you don't give them a device, they will sneak access when you aren't looking. Even the good kids. (We'll talk more about why in the next chapter.) Because of this, we need to keep the lines of communication open. We also need to realize that what we *think* is happening with our kids and social media may not actually be the case. In fact, it probably isn't. They aren't just having harmless fun with friends. I get it. We want to believe the best of our own kids, but we must be open to learn and grow and understand the power of the outside influences they face. We have to be willing to let go of what we thought we knew about any of this.

BUT FIRST, LET'S HUDDLE UP!

Before we go any further down the rabbit hole of the online world, I have a very big "ask" of you as a parent. Please take a few minutes and look at yourself and your approach to parenting and consider how it impacts your child's media usage, and thus their safety online overall. There's an old African proverb that we hear a lot in today's social and political circles; "It takes a village." We need a community of people to help raise well-adjusted kids. But before we look at the "villagers" around your children in the online world, it's critical that the primary caretakers of your child are on the same page. Who else is involved in your child's life? Are you single, married, divorced, or dating? Is there a mentor, coach, teacher, or family member involved in their oversight? It's of the utmost importance that the other caretakers know and agree with the strategic plan for your child's online navigation, and that they are on the same page with you and your child. Trust me, this is a lot easier to do than you think! And yes, by the end of this book, you will have a strategic plan!

CONSIDERATIONS FOR PARENTS:

First, consider your own parenting style and approach to the online world with your kids. What sounds the most like you?

- Do you **forbid** social media and online engagement altogether? Does this include gaming?
- Are you **watching** what your kids are doing online but realize you probably don't know if they have fake accounts or are on platforms you are unaware of?
- Are you **aware** your children are online but feeling confident that they are good kids and will make the right decisions?

- Are you **overwhelmed** by it all and unsure how to handle it?

- Do you think your child's online world and engagement is **their private space** and therefore it wouldn't be right for you to poke around in it?

Now that you've thought through your own style, please ask your coparent. Do you have the same style? Different styles? What about those other mentors in your child's life? What is their take on the topic? And more importantly, do they agree with your style? We need to take an honest look at our own perspective before laying the groundwork for where we are going. This is a critical first step! You need to know the perspective and style of every person making decisions for your child. While I emphatically encourage all caretakers to get on the same page in terms of their approach to the online world, I will say that regardless of your approach, this book has tools for all of you. I promise you will have a plan and have moved mountains when it comes to the safety of your tweens and teens online.

DISPELLING THE MYTHS

Now, let's take a look at some popular myths that I encounter when talking to parents on a regular basis. There's no judgment on parents for where they are coming from. We don't know what we don't know. But if you've bought into any of these myths or made decisions based on them, please consider what I am sharing and be willing to adjust your perspective for the safety of your loved ones. The online world is not at all like the world we live in. The far and dark reaching places of the online world care little for your charming neighborhood. The toxic algorithms and addictive composition of these platforms have zero interest in your family dinners or youth sporting events. The secretive and potentially very dangerous online community that will have access to your child thrives on you resting on these myths.

MYTH 1: "THAT WILL NEVER HAPPEN TO MY KID."

Have you ever thought...

My kid knows better!

But I have great kids!

I live in the best neighborhood, and they go to the best schools!

We have a great family!

My kid is on the honor roll!

They have a great friend group!

I've talked to them about cyberbullying!

I told them not to send inappropriate photos!

They are headed to the college of their dreams!

They made their dream sports team!

CHAPTER ONE

Let me ask you this: Even if the above were true, would you ever consider putting your child on a plane and sending them to a foreign country alone? A country they know nothing about, they don't know the language, they don't know what to expect, they don't know the dangers, they don't know how to get around, they don't know where to stay, they don't know how to contact you...and on top of that, the land is filled with criminals, rapists, drug dealers, and traffickers, and pornography? Would you just send them off because your child really wants to go to a big party there with their friends...completely unsupervised?

Of course you wouldn't. And while that seems like an extreme example. But guess what mom and dad, it's actually not that extreme. In a way, that's exactly what it's like when you hand your child a device or give them access to the online world without preparation. They are exposed to all kinds of real dangers that you could never imagine. They are tempted to do things that are completely out of character. Social pressures combined with the bombardment of temptation can make anyone do things they weren't raised to do and wouldn't normally do. To this point, there's a reality television show on Netflix, *The Push* that explores just how far social pressures can push someone. Shockingly, with little nudges over time, a person can be pushed to do almost anything. Our vulnerable kids are being deeply influenced by the online world, more so than they are being influenced by the offline world. Every kid, even the best of them, is fair game on the myriad of platforms on the internet. My own included. Here I am, the CEO of one of the largest public safety nonprofits, and I talk to my kids about the online world daily. But even I was taken aback when something happened at school pick up one day.

"Mommy, Mommy, want to hear the new version of 'Mary Had a Little Lamb?' Everyone was singing it at recess today and it's so funny!" My nine-year-old beamed as she jumped into the car at carpool. "Sure!" I said. "Can't wait!" Mirroring her enthusiasm. She recited:

Mary had a little lamb
Pop pop bam
The lamb is dead
Posted it on Instagram
It got a lot of likes

Nine years old.

Not on any social media.

Fourth grade.

Great school (not that it matters).

Great neighborhood (not that it matters).

In a community of terrific families (not that it matters).

Caring teachers (not that it matters).

Just a typical Friday recess.

This new version of "Mary Had a Little Lamb" depicts so much of what we know is wrong with the world of social media, shared at such a young age with young, impressionable children. But it also solidifies that it's a reality we cannot ignore. Violence and a general apathy toward the value and sacredness of life—and an exchange for the commodity of "likes"—is creeping in younger and younger.

When a child is exposed to the online world, there is a culmination of many factors that is inherently beyond their developmental maturity. It sucks them up into a weather pattern stronger than they are, more advanced than they are, and for which they are mentally, physically, and emotionally too weak to navigate. The internet will steal your child's innocence. Without question, they will be exposed to things they are too young to see, they will be in contact with people they are too young to manage, and they will receive requests and responses they are too young to make sense of. And yet, a majority of children will still be online, and a majority of parents will let them be, simply because they don't fully understand the dangers or how to manage them, and chalk it up to the "current way of the world."

MYTH #2: "I'LL KEEP MY KID SAFE BY KEEPING THEM OFF THE INTERNET."

I get it and I respect it, but here's the truth; for every ten families I meet who forbid their children from online engagement, nine of them have kids who are online anyway, unbeknownst to the parents and, therefore, completely unmonitored. We know that almost all kids do things behind their parents' backs. I mean, think about it—I'm sure you did as a tween or teen. The problem is that the options now are much more dangerous; your child doesn't have to leave home to engage.

Here's the other problem: Kids are more advanced than their parents when it comes to technology. They will also find ways to get online and connect, including but not limited to:

- Connecting when you are not with them
- Connecting via gadgets owned by others (friends, cousins, grandparents, school gadgets)
- Connecting via the internet and not apps

I've talked to countless parents who do "cell phone checks" to ensure apps like SnapChat, Instagram, etc. are not on their children's phones. I often ask, "How do you know your children are not engaging on these platforms through the old-fashioned world wide web? Or, how do you know your child isn't installing and deleting these apps daily?" "Installing and deleting" sounds like a legitimate nightmare to us, but to them, it's a click here, a click there—two seconds of time.

We have to know this: Their accounts, if created, still exist unless they are actually "deactivated." The username and password still work, with or without an app thumbnail on their home screen.

CHAPTER ONE

Here are some sneaky things our little ones do to gain access without parents knowing: A 2,017-person study done by McAfee found that 70% of teens hide their online behavior from parents.[5] How?

- 53% clear their browser history
- 34% hide or delete instant messages (IMs) or videos
- 21% use an internet-enabled mobile device
- 20% use privacy settings to make content viewable only to friends
- 20% use private browsing modes

Truth: We will never (or almost never) outsmart our teens and tweens when it comes to technology and the online world. So while we will create critical and necessary family rules, and try to learn all we can about the ever-changing online world, a better and lasting strategy is to get kids to buy into what they need to do in order to stay safe while online.

MYTH #3: "MY KID IS SAFE BECAUSE THEIR ACCOUNTS ARE SET TO PRIVATE."

This is a huge misconception, and it fails to take into account one of the most common practices of predators. Once a predator finds a target, he/she will do what they must to engage—and they will be patient. If the target's account is

---

[5] https://www.cnn.com/2012/06/25/tech/web/mcafee-teen-online-survey/index.html

private, this is a sign that this child is more thoughtful about who he/she connects with, so the predator will invest time into researching and forming relationships with others who know your child. They will find connections at school, work, within after-school activities – and spend weeks or months connecting with your child's other friends so that by the time they finally request to connect with your child, they'll have gone from "zero friends in common" to many. As a result, it's more likely that your child will accept the request without hesitation. You might wonder, "How would a predator know who my child's friends are (if their account is private?) or what school or activities they are engaged in?" It's easy. Strangers rely on the whimsical posting of other youth in the circle around your child, but also, they look to you. It's called "sharenting" and it is used when parents share information about their children online. Think of all those parents who post "back to school" spreads each year or share details on every game, award, and birthday. Our social posting impacts the privacy and safety of our children.

A 2010 study found that by the time a child is two years old, 93% have a strong online presence. Their photos, date of birth, body characteristics (tall, short, blond, freckled, etc.), personality, likes and dislikes, pre-school or school, favorite hobbies, and activities all have been shared by us parents. While I absolutely love it when my dear friends share cute kid-related milestones, we must remember that all of this circumvents the privacy we all hope our kids can have online.

CHAPTER ONE

Setting accounts to private offers some level of protection, but it's only step one in making sure our kids are safe. That imaginary boundary wall is easily broken—and broken daily. As soon as they accept connection requests from those unknown to them in real life (think of "friends of friends" or people they do not know but have played games with) they've unlocked the door to their "private" space, mitigating their security. A sad reality is that most kids have already done this.

Beyond that, danger can brew right within their very close community when a friend today turns into an archenemy tomorrow. Among girls who were experiencing cyberbullying, the risk of bullying was seven times higher among current or former friends or dating partners.[6] While that person might be removed or blocked over time, they still have had access to your child's previous posts. Content can and will be taken, controlled, used, and manipulated by others who no longer have our best intentions.

MYTH #4: "MY KID IS SAFE BECAUSE I AM INVOLVED. I FOLLOW THEIR ACCOUNTS AND MONITOR THEIR ACTIVITY."

For those parents who think they've got it covered because they follow their kids accounts, I need you to know that if kids don't want you to see what they're posting, they'll find

---

6 https://www.cbsnews.com/news/teen-cyberbullying-more-likely-from-friends-via-social-media-and-texts/

a way to post it without you knowing. Your presence on one platform simply means they will work hard to post on their other platforms. For example, one strategy for kids is to have "finsta accounts" (fake Instagram accounts) specifically for this reason. Over time, their finsta account becomes their "rinsta" account (real Instagram account) because it will be where their friends really follow them and they share all they really want to share. Additionally, some kids will simply keep posting whatever they want but actively block you from seeing the content. The platforms give them this ability, and kids use it smartly. But don't worry. You are in the right place. This book is about getting to the root of these issues and providing evergreen solutions. A child who understands that you are not trying to limit them but rather protect them from dangers will be more willing to be open and work with you.

MYTH #5: "MY CHILD IS AN INDIVIDUAL WHO DESERVES THEIR ONLINE PRIVACY."

Hopefully this myth has already started to unravel, but parents tell me all the time that they want to respect their child's individual privacy. Please understand, your child's online world is about as private as a glass house in the middle of Times Square. If your child wants to have the privacy to share their thoughts and feelings, or a place to jot down their worries, hopes, crushes, or dreams and express themselves, buy them a diary to keep under their bed with a cute little lock and key. That is private. However, you and they need to accept that nothing online can be considered private. Nothing. When kids share and emote online, they may think they are just "leaning on their friends," but it's like dropping blood in the water for sharks. Predators are looking for kids who are emoting online because they know emotionally vulnerable kids are easy targets. Kids who share their personal content on their phones, with friends or connections, usually unknown to them and you, are setting themselves up for potential disastrous harm.

Remember, your child's smartphone gives them access to the entire world, while at the same time giving the entire world access to your child. It is not a place for privacy, and we, as parents, are mitigating our responsibilities when we ignore this reality. Going back to my opening and somewhat extreme example, not involving yourself in your child's online activity is like dropping them off unprepared in a foreign country alone.

MYTH #6: "I'M SURE THE DIGITAL CONTENT PLATFORMS (SOCIAL MEDIA AND OTHERS) HAVE SAFEGUARDS IN PLACE TO PROTECT CHILDREN SO I DON'T NEED TO WORRY ABOUT IT."

I so wish this myth were true but unfortunately, these companies cater to "eyeballs" and "bottom lines." Sadly, our kids' wellbeing is the price paid for all of it. First, the age requirement to download age-restricted apps is easily thwarted by changing a date of birth, which kids do all the time. There are literally no safeguards or redundancies in place to stop a tween younger than 13 from getting their own Instagram or TikTok account and consuming any type of content. Second, the Wall Street Journal just released a study showing that the algorithms embedded in TikTok will actually feed dangerous content to the user, regardless of their age. In their investigation, a "13-year-old user" searched the term OnlyFans and was immediately able to access pornographic content.[7] Following the search, the 13-year-old user's "ForYou" page on TikTok started to feed the teen a series of sexually oriented videos. In the end, 569 videos on drug use including references to cocaine and meth addiction, as well as promotional videos for the online sales of drug products, were pushed to the 13-year-old user accounts in their investigation. Additionally, over 100 videos promoting pornography sites and sex shops from accounts labeled as "adults only" were also pushed to the young teen account. TikTok's response revealed that the company does not differentiate between videos pushed to adults and children, meaning as long as you are on the platform and are searching for content, their algorithms will strive to make accessing that content easier for you in the future by searching for it and automatically sending it your way, regardless of age. And third, in October of 2021, a Facebook whistleblower testified before Congress reporting that

---

[7] https://www.wsj.com/articles/tiktok-algorithm-sex-drugs-minors-11631052944?mod=hp_lead_pos5

CHAPTER ONE

Facebook routinely chose profit over safety even though the mega-app had data showing certain aspects of the platform were harmful. Why do they do this? As I said before, it's about eyeballs and money. How do they get away with it? Section 230 of the Communications Decency Act holds digital companies harmless—for now. So much needs to change.

MYTH #7: "IT'S ALL TOO MUCH TO KEEP UP WITH. KIDS WILL DO WHAT KIDS WILL DO."

Ok, maybe that's not entirely a myth. But the idea that you can't do anything about it is a myth. Some parents look away from technology and what their kids are doing online because it all just seems too overwhelming. Many of us can barely keep up with our own social accounts, let alone monitor and track our child, or two, or three, or four (or more) children. But that's exactly why I put together this book. For the sake of our kids, we have to. Once you understand the four tools, you can discuss them and set up boundaries as a family. You don't have to keep up with every single new app or social slang that's out there. Also, we must rely on tools that are created to help parents—artificial intelligence parental monitoring programs like "BARK" can provide support. The point is, together, we'll teach our kids evergreen principles that apply across all platforms, and there are additional tools to help. You can do this! I promise! We'll do it together.

I also realize this may feel like a fire hose of information and we are just in the first chapter. I've asked a lot of you as a parent. I've invited you to open up and trust me, a total stranger for all intents and purposes, and also to be willing to admit that what you've thought may be wrong, and the way you've approached your kids and the online world may have to change. Parenting is not for the faint of heart. Parenting in the digital age is "next-level" complex, so I commend you for taking this journey with me on behalf of your child and family. I promise you will not regret it. And although your mind may be blown as we keep digging deeper, we will put it all back together again before we are done. So take a deep breath, grab some coffee or tea or your drink of choice, and let's move on to the next chapter where we will explore your child's inner world. Yes, there's a perfectly logical explanation for why your kid, and all kids, go completely off the rails at times.

CHAPTER 2

Your Child's Developing Inner World

Given that the brain's deep emotional centers are "hijacking the ship" at this stage, their good decision-making ability shouldn't be relied upon as the norm.

It's no secret that children navigate major developmental milestones at the same time they are navigating the online world. Adolescence is an enormous time of growth and change. Our kids go through physical, mental, emotional, and social changes. Cognitively, they start to think abstractly, develop questions, think long term, and form empathy for others. They also go from complete dependence on you to independence. The road through all of this is not necessarily a smooth or easy one. Kids are hardwired to push away from their parents during this time, but they still desperately crave, and need, the safety of loving boundaries and guidance that only parents and caretakers can provide.

Researchers suggest that most of these changes fall within three primary developmental stages of adolescence and young adulthood: early adolescence, middle adolescence, and late adolescence/young adulthood. While within those

CHAPTER TWO

years there are many developmental changes we could focus on. I'd like to zero in on two–puberty and brain development.[8] The beginning of adolescence occurs around the onset of puberty. It is marked by dramatic changes in hormone levels and in physical characteristics, including rapid physical growth, changes in facial structure, and the appearance of secondary sexual characteristics. On average, girls begin puberty between eight and 11 years of age and boys between 10 and 13 years of age. Even a mature child, one who has gone through puberty early or seems socially more responsible than others, will make careless decisions during this time. All kids do. Didn't you? And if there's a story from your past you feel comfortable sharing with your kids, please do so. It will go a long way in helping them understand their own development.

It is critical to know that during this time of puberty, a child faces more than physical changes. There are tremendous emotional changes taking place along with issues with self-confidence. For example, one study found that when puberty sets in, a sharp decline in confidence takes place, negatively impacting personalities. Between the ages of eight and 14, the "rate of confidence" drops in both girls and boys, but the most significant drop was reported in girls, who showed a 30% decrease. Can you imagine what it feels like for them to navigate the online world during this time?

---

[8] https://www.theatlantic.com/family/archive/2018/09/puberty-girls-confidence/563804/

While the body goes through physical changes starting as young as eight years old in girls and ten years old in boys, critical brain development is also taking place. Most importantly, I want to draw attention to the area of the brain called the prefrontal cortex. This is the part of the brain that monitors impulse control, planning, and future orientation, which is the ability to consider consequences. While in a developing state, this part of the brain causes kids to be more responsive to rewards than to punishment. So a pubescent child will make choices that seem like a really good idea in the moment based on a perceived reward, without ever considering what will happen as a result. If you ask them why they did what they did, they'll say, "I don't know!" and they aren't lying. They're driven by impulse. So, while physically they are developing to look like adults, their psychosocial, cognitive, and social development (which helps them self-regulate), is developing at a much slower rate and continues to develop into their mid-20s. These deeply rooted changes speak to the reason why many teenagers seek thrills, break rules, and seem nonchalant about their own safety. And, most significant for the purposes of this book, the disconnect among what a teen or preteen feels physically, what they process cognitively, and what they feel emotionally becomes really critical when faced with the complexities of the online world. But there's even more to this period of physical and brain development that we need to be aware of, especially when thinking about tweens and teens (and even young adults) who replace so much time with technology.

CHAPTER TWO

IQ, PRUNING, AND DEVELOPMENTAL DELAYS

Scientists now know that structural changes in an adolescent's brain affect the choices they will make, as well as, potentially, their IQ over time. Also, it is interesting to note that there are actual pathways in the brain that when not being used over time, will be pruned! I don't know about you but I find it incredible to think about! Children who spend hours on gadgets and cut out things like critical thinking and reading could be limiting their use of those skills later in life. Knowing this, we will serve them well if we can replace some online time with quality time reading, creating, playing and enjoying time outdoors.[9]

Our movement as a culture away from healthy habits such as physical movement, touch, human connection, and nature,[10] and toward technology-centered living has affected our young children in a negative way. The past decade has seen an unprecedented increase in referrals to occupational therapists for writing and reading delays, attention and learning difficulties, and significant behavior problems in children. Knowing what we know, parents, it's our responsibility to create balance for our growing children. While we cannot remove all technology, we also cannot allow technology to replace the natural stimulants the world provides to support healthy development.

---

9   https://www.youtube.com/watch?v=MHs7vlcwRXY
10 http://www.sensomotorische-integratie.nl/CrisRowan.pdf

BRAIN DEVELOPMENT, EMOTIONS, AND DECISION-MAKING

The way that different brain regions "talk" to one another in teenagers may explain their sometimes confounding behavior. Adolescents have the ability to make quick, efficient, and correct decisions which leads us to trust them. However, the brain's deep emotional centers are "hijacking the ship" at this stage, so their good decision-making ability shouldn't be relied upon as the norm. While scientists typically refer to the teenage brain as 13 to 17 year-olds, many of us look at the decisions of our 20-year-olds and really scratch our heads!

Here's why: That prefrontal cortex, and its connections to other areas of the brain don't fully develop until the age of 25. Let's also remember that for our tweens and teens, a number of deep structures in the brain are influenced by changes in hormones associated with puberty, which all lead to heightened emotions, impulsive decision-making, and a heavy focus on rewards. Surprise! Add all of this up and we can clearly see causes for concern when a child is facing complicated decisions in the online world.

BRAIN DEVELOPMENT AND HABITS

Teens are rapid learners since their brains are still developing (Ever notice how quickly a young mind can learn a language?). But all of this means that, sadly, they can get addicted faster, longer, and stronger[11] because addiction is related to learning and memory. This also explains why so many tweens and teens literally cannot put their gadgets down. In fact, one study shows that over 54% of US teens feel they spend too much time on their phones. Many are studying the world of technology addiction.[12]

Understanding the powerful impact behind the physical and emotional changes during puberty and the decision-making and impulse control issues related to brain development, top researchers rely on functional magnetic resonance imaging to monitor brain development and study brain activity specifically during this time. Parents and caretakers, if you can't quite figure out your teen, rest assured you are in good company! One of the biggest take-home messages behind all this "sciency stuff" is that during a time when critical parts of our children's brains and personalities are developing, our kids are also extremely sensitive to rewards and seek to find them in any, if not all, situations or activities. And here is what every parent and caretaker needs to understand: That innate drive for "reward" has a much larger meaning, significance, and impact in the online world; which is why the nexus between "online use" and the developing tween/teen brain is so incredibly important to understand.

---

11 Dr. Frances Jensen, https://thechart.blogs.cnn.com/2011/04/22/tedmed-young-brains-autism-and-epilepsy/
12 https://www.pewresearch.org/fact-tank/2019/08/23/most-u-s-teens-who-use-cellphones-do-it-to-pass-time-connect-with-others-learn-new-things/

THE POWER OF THE REWARD SYSTEM
AND ONLINE THREATS

So, what is a reward? A reward is any type of payoff for a behavior, be it a coin in a game, a "like" on a photo, or a compliment from a friend or crush. When teenagers are in "packs" or with friends, the reward system of the brain gets even more aroused and becomes a driving force. They'd rather impress their friends than worry about any potential risk associated with their wellbeing or even survival. They simply and intentionally place greater value on the reward.[13] Soon, I'll walk you through "online challenges" that create unimaginable risks and what we are discussing here, helps us understand why our kids engage in such activities to begin with.

Consider this story: It was 3 a.m. in a small town in North Carolina, and there wasn't a lot for a group of teenagers to do. Hillary, her brother, and three other guys sneaked out of their homes and broke into a private pool down the street to go skinny dipping. Two days later, a policeman showed up at Hillary's house after some of the friends bragged about the trespassing and skinny-dipping adventure. Hillary and her brother went to court and were convicted. Their mother paid the fine. "Sometimes I wonder where their brains are," Hillary's mother said. "They do such impulsive things, and

---
13 https://www.cnn.com/2011/10/19/health/mental-health/teen-brain-impulses/index.html

CHAPTER TWO

sometimes I just don't think they're thinking."[14] She is right. These kids chose to sneak out of their house, at 3 a.m., break into a private facility, trespass, go swimming, and brag about it later to their other friends. None of it makes sense to us (or even sounds fun, to be honest) but understanding brain development and puberty, the desire for thrills, risks and rewards, plus the added bonus of peer pressure and peer thinking—we start to understand.

REWARDS AND DRUGS AND ALCOHOL

The reward-seeking brains of teens may also lead them to experiment with pleasure-inducing substances like drugs and alcohol, which are especially dangerous for this age group. Because vital structures in the teen brain are still developing, adolescents are more prone to brain damage from drugs and alcohol use. Research has shown that teenagers who binge drink will have greater brain damage than adults engaging in the same behavior.[15] Marijuana can stay in a person's system for days, impacting the building blocks of learning and memory. That's likely because the teen brain has more receptors open for drugs to bind to, and the same is true for alcohol. Add this understanding to the overwhelming reality that the online world offers tweens and teens a multitude of options when it comes to drugs (both in variety and in ease

---

14 https://tbilawyers.com/blog/are-teenagers-wired-differently/
15 https://thechart.blogs.cnn.com/2010/11/15/teen-brain-more-prone-to-drug-alcohol-damage/

of purchase) and this becomes an area of grave concern.

PARENTING THE TEENAGE BRAIN IN AN ONLINE WORLD

There are entire books written on this topic for good reason. This can be the most challenging time for parents. Changing the "hardwired" reward-seeking tendencies of teenagers is difficult, but we can restructure the environment in a way that makes things safer for our tweens and teens.

Parents, here are some pointers on how to do this:

- Make sure kids don't spend a lot of time unsupervised and find creative and fun ways to spend time with them. The goal here is to move away from trying to micromanage them to actually spending time together.

- Enroll teens in healthy after-school programs where adults are present.

- Keep them busy. Keep their minds engaged in something, keep their bodies active via sports, dance, or even weekly neighborhood walks.

- Get to know their friends, their social world, and what makes them feel confident, happy, scared, and insecure.

- Teens learn from other teens. Get your teen around kids who have the same values you do.

- Understand that they want to hear from you even though they make it seem like they do not.

CHAPTER TWO

- Reward good behavior. Tap into those reward-seeking tendencies and use the force for good! Use incentives to keep them motivated, whatever those incentives mean for you and your family!

THE DEVELOPING BRAIN, GAMING, DIGITAL STREAMING

My generation grew up loving Saturday morning cartoons. It was the best day of the week for boys and girls across the country. Today's cartoons are very different from the cartoons from just a decade ago. Current studies find that after just nine minutes of viewing today's fast-paced TV cartoons, kids experience an immediate decrease in cognitive and executive function.[16] Yes. Read that again. The result of this hinders abstract thinking, short-term memory, and impulse control in preschoolers. It's not about how much kids watch; it's what they watch. Certain shows compromise their ability to learn and use self-control immediately after watching; what a detriment for our children! The young human brain isn't equipped to process things that happen at such a surreal speed. It becomes exhausting to their brains.[17]

Beyond the impact of screen time on the developing mind, it's important to look at the impact of violence in media and gaming as well on brain development and behaviors. Here is some interesting, and alarming, research.

---

16 https://pediatrics.aappublications.org/content/128/4/644
17 https://abcnews.go.com/Health/Wellness/watching-spongebob-makes-preschoolers-slower-thinkers-study-finds/story?id=14482447

VIOLENCE IN MEDIA

I have had many conversations with experts on the impact violence in the media has on youth. Experts disagree on the impact, and there are even studies that say there is none. However, we know when our children sit with something long enough, it starts to affect their personality.

I'll also share with you this fun fact: As the usage of gun violence in TV programming grew (between 2000 and 2018), so did gun use in the US. We saw criminal activity reflect this with homicide numbers climbing.[18] We also saw more children pick up weapons and use them, leading us to further examine the relationship between the content kids view and the impact it has on their development, and ultimately the choices they make.

GAMING AND VIOLENCE

When it comes to gaming, we look at the impact of violence as well as that of fast-paced technologies, 3-D imaging, and something called "game transfer phenomena." Let's look at violence in gaming first. Here the data is a bit more transparent. Studies that looked at hundreds of kids seventh to ninth grade (ages 11–14) focused on the effects of violent video game habits on adolescent hostility, aggressive behaviors, and school performance. It found that adolescents exposed to greater amounts of video game violence were

---

18 https://www.sciencedaily.com/releases/2021/03/210317141625.htm

CHAPTER TWO

more hostile. It was reported they get into arguments with teachers more frequently, and are more likely to be involved in physical fights, while also performing more poorly in school as a result.[19] Many now agree that there is a casual risk factor between young minds exposed to violent video games and increased aggressive behavior and aggressive thinking. It also appears that these young minds show decreased empathy for others.[20] And of course, in addition to being exposed to violence in gaming, a high proportion of boys eight to 10 years old are playing games intended for 18-year-olds and they are being exposed to violence and sexual content not appropriate for their age.[21]

Impact of fast-paced technologies. What about the effect of fast-paced technologies on our children—things like gaming, or constant scrolling through ten-second videos, or constantly swiping? Many have asked me if the consumption of fast-paced imagery and content leads to attention deficit disorder, impatience, or the lack of ability to concentrate or focus. The answer is unequivocally yes. Science has in fact found that children who overuse fast-paced technologies are "pruning" their brains (cutting or removing unused pathways) and thereby hindering access to their frontal lobes, which we've discussed is the center for executive function and impulse control. Additional reports

---

19 Gentile et.al., 2004 https://screenstrong.com/are-video-games-making-our-kids-violent/
20 Moore, 2010 https://screenstrong.com/are-video-games-making-our-kids-violent/
21 https://cybersafeireland.org/blog/posts/2019/september/cybersafeireland-releases-its-4th-annual-report/

show that modern technology does reduce attention span and increases distractibility, while at the same time hindering a child's ability to interact socially with others in person and in real time.[22]

GAME TRANSFER PHENOMENA

I've thought about this before and I would imagine that you have too. You look at kids playing video games and the visuals seem so real, and the sounds so incredibly piercing. Some gadgets even allow for vibration through the thumbstick or game controller, adding to what the player is seeing, hearing, feeling, and thus experiencing. Studies have examined this too and discovered that a real phenomenon takes place called Game Transfer. This is when a player (our kids) transfers what they see, hear, and consume (the killing and aggressive violence) from the virtual world to the real world. Once all the senses are engaged, the brain doesn't know the difference between fantasy and reality. This phenomenon impacts 30-40% of gamers, raising the question of a potential tie between gaming and mass killings.[23]

---

22 https://code.likeagirl.io/fast-changing-tech-and-how-it-affects-your-brain-477b461c64b7?gi=6e96df4eeb4c
23 (Ortiz de Gortari, Aronsson, & Griffiths, 2011, Ortiz de Gortari & Griffiths, 2014)

CHAPTER TWO

3-D GAMING: IMPACT ON ANGER

And what about feelings of increased anger when players spend a lot of time on such real and improved video gaming technology? A link between anger and aggression and playing video games has been found, but the question remains whether that tie is due to a child feeding off the aggression of the game, or simply expressing frustration spending time on a game that is difficult.[24]

WHEN DO KIDS DIFFERENTIATE REALITY FROM FANTASY?

So while people argue over these things (why, I don't know) we do know there are consequences to consuming digital content as well as consuming aggressive content and violent video games. However, I think there is more we need to examine. Have you ever sat with a child who's spent a lot of time building a world, home, or city in Minecraft or playing with friends (or strangers) in Roblox? If you listen to them talk—if you *really listen*—you might start to wonder if these kids know the difference between reality and fantasy. Even if they literally know the difference between what's real and fake, the impact of that fake world in their real lives is quite significant. What is the impact of fantasy and make-believe on a developing adolescent's mind and emotions? This is important to consider. My middle child can spend hours

---

[24] https://www.researchgate.net/publication/230326504_The_Effect_of_Violent_Videogame_Playtime_on_Anger

building entire cities in these games and then spend time being crushed when those creations are destroyed. She knows it's a game. She knows it's not real, but the impact of loss or changes within that fantasy world affects her literally in real time and in real life.

It is important to know the difference between fantasy and reality when many of our kids "live" in fantasy spaces. We know that children between the ages of two and three begin to understand the categories of what's real and what's fake and can use cues to fit things into real (horse, fish) and unreal (unicorn, mermaid) categories. By age 12, that process has been firmly developed.[25] But because the prefrontal cortex is not fully developed until age 25, there are young adults who are deeply impacted by unreal things taking place in gaming or fantasy platforms. We need to recognize this and help them manage this disconnect. And it's not hard. We can shine a light on the issue through conversations and guidelines. Most kids carry around the consequences of what happens in the online world as if it is their real life. A fantasy world built on Minecraft or in Roblox (for example) impacts a child's real feelings, opinions, moods, and thoughts. We need to pay attention to how it impacts their real life, why it influences them in this way, and help them come back to reality. We need to help them find balance. During this critical time of development, children are already filled with emotional extremes, and managing the consequences of

---

25 https://liberalarts.utexas.edu/psychology/faculty/profile.php?eid=jwoolley

both the real world and a fantasy world can be overwhelming. Adults have the capacity to manage this and create balance, but youth do not. Beyond conversations, kids need guidelines. When or if you choose to place rules or limits on gaming devices and streaming content (and I hope you do) share your reasons why you are doing so. Present the facts and concerns as best as you can, in an age-appropriate manner that gives them understanding, a level of control, and makes them part of the decision regarding rules and limits. I explain how to do this in the coming chapters and provide questions and conversation starters for you. I am a firm believer that we must arm our children with a road map—giving them the rules based on knowledge, understanding, and buy in so that they will keep those guidelines by choice, wherever they go in their digital worlds.

CHAPTER 3

Welcome to the Online Jungle

When you give your child access to the online world, you give the world access to your child.

Ok parents, great job taking the wakeup call about what's happening online. Here's where things are about to really hit home. So far, we've broad-stroked what happens online, we've explored the most common myths, you've looked at yourself, your beliefs, and your parenting style, and we've looked at the critical biology and brain development of teens and young adults. Deep breath! Now, we are going deeper. It's time to look behind the veil of the digital world and start "dissecting" this online jungle. To do that, we must look at how Covid has changed the online world for all of us.

In 2019, prior to Covid, there were 328.2 million people in America and 7.674 billion people in the world. But how many were online? In looking at a few of the top social media platforms, you'll see the numbers are staggering.

2020 numbers for Twitter indicate the platform had 192 million daily active users and a reachable audience of

CHAPTER THREE

353 million users[26]. Sixty-three percent of all Twitter users worldwide were between ages 35 and 65, and the ratio of female to male users was roughly one to two: 34% female and 66% male.[27]

2020 numbers for Facebook indicate the platform had 1.69 billion users.[28] That number has grown to an estimated 2.8 billion.[29]

2020 numbers for SnapChat indicate the platform had roughly 265 million daily active users worldwide. 59% of all U.S. internet users ages 13 to 24 use SnapChat. Over 210 million snaps are created on SnapChat every day.[30]

2020 numbers for Instagram indicate the platform had roughly one billion monthly active users and 500 million people used Instagram stories daily. About 71% of U.S. adults between the ages of 18-29 are using Instagram. As of 2020, 52% of Instagram's audience identified as female and 48% identified as male.[31] Approximately 72% of teenagers in the United States use Instagram.[32]

2020 numbers for TikTok indicate it was installed on devices over 2.6 billion times worldwide. With its base doubling nearly yearly, as of this writing, installations are expected to be well beyond 3 billion.[33]

---

26 https://adespresso.com/blog/instagram-statistics/
27 https://www.oberlo.com/blog/twitter-statistics
28 https://www.statista.com/statistics/490424/number-of-worldwide-facebook-users/
29 https://adespresso.com/blog/instagram-statistics/
30 https://www.oberlo.com/blog/SnapChat-statistics
31 https://www.statista.com/statistics/730315/instagram-stories-dau/
32 https://adespresso.com/blog/instagram-statistics/
33 https://influencermarketinghub.com/tiktok-stats/

And a quick look at Pinterest, Fortnite, and Roblox showed 2020 numbers at 459 million users,[34] 350 million gamers,[35] and over 164 million players,[36] respectively.

A newer site, and one of huge concern, OnlyFans, has roughly 30 million registered users and more than 450,000 content creators. As of 2020, the site had paid out more than $600 million to its content creators.[37]

So here's the deal, there are millions and millions of users on the platforms our kids are on daily. We looked at the impact of violence and fast-paced technology on adolescents through TV, digital streaming, and video games, but how does online usage, in general, impact kids?

Well, the impact is staggering. Prior to Covid, the biggest issues were:

- The amount of time kids spent consuming content
- The number of kids talking to strangers online
- The mental impact social media was having on youth

Here is a quick look at the issues pre-Covid. Already, our kids were consuming content like never before. In fact, the number of American youth who were watching online videos daily was doubling in kids ages eight to 18 prior to Covid. Pre-Covid numbers showed that almost 60% of kids eight

---

34 https://adespresso.com/blog/instagram-statistics/
35 https://backlinko.com/epic-games-users
36 https://www.gamepur.com/guides/how-many-people-play-roblox
37 https://influencermarketinghub.com/what-is-OnlyFans/

to 12 years old and 70% of kids 13 to 18 years old watched online videos daily.[38] The consumption of digital content means the amount of time youth spent on social media was also increasing. Pre-Covid, some teens were spending up to nine hours a day on social media platforms, with 30% of that time designated to socializing with others. Most of this online engagement was achieved on mobile devices like a cell phone.[39]

Considering all of the brain and developmental impacts we just explored, add the reality that almost half of kids eight to 13 years old pre-Covid, reported talking to strangers online, with 33% of those kids talking to strangers every day or at least once a week.[40] They do it knowingly.

And of course, many experts at the time were diving into the correlation between teenagers who spend more than three hours a day on social media and the development of mental health problems including depression, anxiety, aggression, and antisocial behavior.

Those were the issues *prior* to Covid. Once Covid hit, however, it created an entirely new set of issues. Not only did it increase the number of users, but it also changed our kids' online usage habits. Regardless of the state of Covid in the future, those new habits are here to stay.

---

38 https://internetsafety101.org/mobilestatistics Common Sense Media, October 29, 2019
39 https://www.socialmediatoday.com/marketing/how-much-time-do-people-spend-social-media-infographic
40 https://cybersafeireland.org/blog/posts/2019/september/cybersafeireland-releases-its-4th-annual-report/

COVID'S IMPACT

The Covid restrictions have done a number on our children. Yes, Covid took the lives of many adults, but it waged war of a different kind against children and adolescents. How? An overwhelming majority reported having increased screen time thanks to boredom. It's affected friendships, education, as well as health, hunger, vision, sleep, and obesity in a record number of children. It's changed the way children engage and interact and socialize online, leading to a huge increase in the online solicitation of minors, as well as exposure to online violence and pornography, sexting, and more. Whether we like it or not, this is a new reality and the new foundation moving forward.

LIFE ONLINE

The most obvious change in online usage due to Covid has to do with the unprecedented rise in screen time. Whether due to school closures, lockdowns, or boredom, all of the sudden classrooms, socializing, entertainment, exercising, and most other activities were replaced with technology and digital tools. The effects permeate everything and are everlasting.

We have already shown that screen time was trending up pre-Covid. Post-Covid, it skyrocketed, and not just in children eight and over but also in children age four and over. The time children spent on platforms like YouTube, for example, doubled between February of 2020 and March/

CHAPTER THREE

April of that same year.[41] This was time they were spending online due to boredom. But this doubling of time online due to boredom was separate and distinct from the time they were spending online for schooling or socializing.

EFFECTS ON FAMILY

If family life was relatively normal pre-Covid, we know a lot of that changed post-Covid. The pressure, financial stress, and isolation caused by the pandemic wreaked havoc on families and couples, causing children (many for the first time) to witness and absorb changes in the family dynamic. These children's sense of personal joy, security, and stability were shaken. Add to this that some children saw a lot of violence between domestic partners. Children and family pets were also hurt as a result. Additionally, the onset of drug and alcohol use went up across the country.[42] Children began experimenting with drugs and alcohol more as well.[43]

EFFECTS ON FRIENDSHIPS

Beyond the increased time online, the boredom, and the changes within family dynamics were the changes in kids'

---

41 https://internetsafety101.org/mobilestatistics
42 https://health.ucsd.edu/news/releases/Pages/2021-08-24-how-adolescents-used-drugs-during-the-Covid-19-pandemic.aspx
43 https://jamanetwork.com/journals/jamanetworkopen/fullarticle/2770975

social circles. Children, most not mature enough to deal with these issues, were soon navigating major changes affecting the very core of all they knew up until this time. So how did social circles change? In many ways. Young friends didn't see each other for a long time. With the new option of remote or virtual learning, you had social groups within single school communities become fractured. One group of kids returned to school and shared these historic moments together, face-to-face or mask-to-mask. Other friends, within the same friend group, were isolated at home because a parent or caretaker chose for them to be a virtual student.

EFFECTS ON EDUCATION

With more than 1.5 billion children and young people affected by school closures worldwide,[44] the effects on education are still yet to be fully known. But here's what we have started to uncover—children went back to school in masks and shields while others stayed home. You had local politicians and federal officials fighting over protocols, leaving school officials, and our children, in the middle. At the onset, schools struggled to teach students remotely. Students struggled with limited internet access, inconsistent online procedures, and difficulties following virtually or catching up. Then there were also many children embarrassed by their home environment and doing everything they could to "save face" or

---

44 https://www.unicef.org/romania/press-releases/children-increased-risk-harm-online-during-global-Covid-19-pandemic-unicef

choose an absence over participating in a virtual school session that invited their entire class into their home or bedroom. Students in many grade levels are now believed to be, on average, five to ten percentile points behind (2020 vs 2019).[45] Additional data shows minority and less-affluent students fell three to five months behind while white students fell one to three months behind.[46] And there's more. In parts of California for example, the number of elementary students absent increased by more than 200%.[47] At one point, there were an estimated 3 million vulnerable students (homeless, in foster care, with disabilities or learning English) who were not in school at all.[48] Steep declines in attendance, a rising number of failing grades, and shrinking enrollment caused great concern over dropout rates, nationally. There's no question, dealing with Covid greatly interfered with our children's right to learn and thrive in school.

EFFECTS ON MENTAL HEALTH, VISION, AND HUNGER

The global death toll due to Covid is still changing. But beyond death, it impacts all of us through the push to online living, the mitigation of social engagement, the onset of fear, the

---

45   https://www.nbcnews.com/news/education/when-Covid-19-closed-schools-black-hispanic-poor-kids-took-n1249352
46   https://www.mckinsey.com/industries/public-and-social-sector/our-insights/Covid-19-and-learning-loss-disparities-grow-and-students-need-help
47   https://www.the74million.org/article/the-numbers-are-ugly-chronic-absenteeism-among-california-elementary-students-could-be-surging-by-more-than-200-percent/
48   https://bellwethereducation.org/publication/missing-margins-estimating-scale-Covid-19-attendance-crisis

polarization of groups, the hyper-infusion of politics, and more.

The results: An increase in depression, anxiety, and a tremendous amount of fear.[49] Within the first 10 months of the pandemic, emergency rooms had seen a 24% increase in mental health-related visits from children ages five to 11 when compared to the same time period pre-Covid. The rise in emergency room visits among older kids was even higher at 31%.[50]

What about the impact on vision? There's been an alarming rise in people with myopia (nearsightedness) associated with potentially blinding complications such as glaucoma, retinal detachment, and myopic macular degeneration. Experts attribute this rise to the overuse of handheld devices.[51] Children are particularly vulnerable to developing myopia because their eyes are still developing and are constantly on gadgets. With so many children experiencing the same vision problems, many parents see the onset of nearsightedness as "normal."[52] While myopia is irreversible, research also shows that limiting gadget time and adding time outdoors is a simple way to reduce the risk of developing myopia and its progression in adolescents.

---

49 https://www.ncbi.nlm.nih.gov/pmc/articles/PMC7444649/
50 https://www.cdc.gov/mmwr/volumes/69/wr/mm6945a3.htm#:~:text=Beginning%20in%20April%202020%2C%20the,17%20years%20increased%20approximately%2024%25
51 American Academy of Ophthalmology (2014), 42% of the U.S. population has myopia, a sharp increase
52 Myopia Control Clinic at UC Berkeley's School of Optometry (Dr. Liu, 2013)

CHAPTER THREE

Food banks were also slammed with hungry families as an estimated 17 million children—many largely cut off from free school lunches—are now in danger of not having enough to eat. That's an increase of more than six million hungry children compared to before the pandemic.[53]

ONLINE SOCIAL INTERACTIONS

With students spending more time online, the side effects are staggering. We will explore these in depth in chapters eight and nine, but most concerning is the number of children at risk for online sexual exploitation and grooming. With more kids online, spending more time engaging with more people, coupled with boredom, curiosity, and a lack of face-to-face contact with friends, we see kids choosing to engage in heightened-risk activities. These activities range from sending sexualized images, to surfing dark parts of the online world and engaging with explicit, harmful, and violent content. Parents, also navigating these stressful pandemic times, were not supervising digital screen time.

Often alone in the online space, we saw cyberbullying, hate speech, and online toxicity increase. Whether kids were commenting on Twitter, TikTok, or engaging on an increased number of platforms from FaceTime, Zoom, Google Classroom, Moodle, Canvas, Web-ex, BlackBoard, or others, we saw kids simply become "meaner."

---

53 https://www.feedingamericaaction.org/the-impact-of-coronavirus-on-food-insecurity/

PORNOGRAPHY/SEXTING

At the onset of Covid, nearly 40% of children had either received or sent a "sext" (a text message with sexually explicit or suggestive images, messages, or videos) by the age of 13.[54] Boredom and idle time (thanks to the pandemic), plus increased online access has increased the availability and interest in sexually driven content. Access to pornography is real and, might I say, terrifying. According to Pornhub, more than 5,824,699,200 hours of porn were watched in 2019 alone.[55] That's equal to almost 665 calendar years of content consumed in one year, on just one porn site. This is pre-Covid. For those on the site, the most searched terms were "lesbian," "teen," "stepmom," "mom," and "stepsister."[56] With the onset of the pandemic, consumption and exploitation only continued to increase and, in some cases, consumption of this type of material is becoming a new normal for our children.

Those most-searched terms really leave me asking about the impact of this industry on women and children. Overall, we are seeing an early onset of pornography addiction, with children as young as eight being exposed. We see erectile dysfunction increasing and more reports of aggressiveness in dating. We hear that those who consume a high volume of pornographic content need their young partners to

---
54 https://blog.jiminy.me/2019/12/17/children-and-sexting-a-jiminy-report/
55 https://fightthenewdrug.org/2019-pornhub-annual-report/
56 https://fightthenewdrug.org/2019-pornhub-annual-report/

engage in offensive and abusive sex acts, just to feel satisfied. Data reveals that self-generated imagery now accounts for nearly a third of web pages featuring sexual images of children. More than three quarters of the self-generated materials, whether images or videos, feature children 11 to 13 years old, a majority of which are female.[57] This means that during the pandemic, demand for this type of content has increased and more children are creating it easily from home. Predators and businesses are "cashing in" as they distribute the material in plain sight to various everyday platforms.

According to a recent report published in JAMA Pediatrics, one in four kids will admit to sexting.[58] Word on the street is that sexting is the new "first base."[59] But how many have been asked for nude photos? By age 13, 24% of children were asked at some point to send nude photos. Those numbers were generally higher for girls. As many as 6.8% of 10-year-old girls having been asked for nude photos. But overall, the numbers found that sexting among kids and teens is mostly mutual, with 58.5% of all sexts being sent between two willing parties for kids ages 10 to 17.[60] Why does this happen? Constant access to a device. Hormones. Peer pressure. Curiosity. If your kid isn't participating, chances are, they have a friend who is.

---

[57] Internet Watch Foundation, Jan. 15, 2020) https://internetsafety101.org/mobilestatistics
[58] https://time.com/5172906/sexting-messages-teens/
[59] https://www.washingtonpost.com/news/parenting/wp/2014/10/06/sexting-is-the-new-first-base-yes-maybe-even-your-child/
[60] https://www.google.com/amp/s/nypost.com/2019/12/17/over-40-of-kids-are-exposed-to-sexting-by-age-14-survey-finds/amp/

Things to keep in mind: Sending an unsolicited nude photo is a form of sexual harassment. It's serious and taken seriously. Receiving nude photos of a minor classifies as being in possession of child pornography. Just having it on your phone, even if you don't share it is bad enough. Sharing a nude photo of a minor is classified as distributing child pornography, an absolute crime. Because the content is digital, it can be screenshot and/or sent to anywhere and to anyone in seconds. Naked pictures of minors are illegal and can be considered child pornography, even if it's two children willingly exchanging them. Sexting laws vary from state to state. Some jurisdictions have "Romeo and Juliet" provisions, which lessen the severity of the offense when the parties involved are similar in age. It's important to talk to your kids about this and know the laws in your state.

At the same time, reports of child sexual exploitation activity to cyber-tip hotlines are up by an average of 30% globally.[61] Domestically, reports to the National Center for Missing and Exploited Children, the organization that receives cyber-tips in the United States, including from all of the Silicon Valley technology platforms, have more than doubled, from 983,734 reports in March 2019 to 2,027,520 reports March 2020.[62] A smaller number of videos that went viral contributed to this significant rise in new reports.

---

61 https://www.nbcnews.com/tech/tech-news/child-sexual-abuse-images-online-exploitation-surge-during-pandemic-n1190506
62 https://www.nbcnews.com/tech/tech-news/child-sexual-abuse-images-online-exploitation-surge-during-pandemic-n1190506

THE GOOD NEWS

Not every impact of Covid has been negative. Juvenile arrests and incarcerations trended down during the pandemic. This could be a combination of "stay-at-home" orders coupled with criminal justice reform sweeping the nation. You might be thinking, "Okay, I've had enough. I'm throwing all gadgets away and moving to a bunker somewhere." If you are freaked out right now, it's normal and you should be. But stick with me, I have some solutions and strategies that are easy to implement, evergreen, and will carry us through.

CHAPTER 4

It's Time We Had a Talk: Mentally Preparing Your Child

As you navigate whether your tween or teen is ready for a smartphone, conversations about all the issues they may encounter must be discussed with them in a strategic way.

Every October, I find myself talking about Halloween safety. I'm often asked, "How do I know if my child is old enough or mature enough to trick or treat alone?" My answer is always the same, "That depends on how they would handle the conversation around the issues that could come up."

So, here's my advice on this topic: If your kid wanted to trick or treat alone, you would have a few safety conversations with them before they go, wouldn't you? Take for example, pedestrian safety. It's essential to talk about how to cross streets safely. You would tell them to be careful to not get hit or killed by a car, bus, or train. You would remind them that Halloween is the worst night of the year for pedestrian accidents. You'll tell them to stay with their friend group so they don't get lost, hurt, or placed in danger alone. You'll tell them they need to come home before a certain time, because there is greater danger being out too late and alone.

CHAPTER FOUR

We tell kids not to take dark back roads or go off the beaten path, because if they do, they may find themselves alone or followed, or in a place they are unfamiliar with, where you can't keep an eye on them, or simply where they are not safe. You'll ask them to keep their phone on and charged so you can reach them or make sure they can reach you...I could go on and on.

Here's the thing: If you had a child who was absolutely freaked out by this conversation and the dangers of Halloween, that's an indication the child is not ready for the inherent responsibilities of going trick or treating alone. Now, if you know this about your child and choose not to talk to them about these safety issues and still allow them to go out, you are essentially and potentially setting them up for failure or harm. Instead of talking to them about a potential risk and ensuring they are prepared and can pull from a tool belt of solutions, you will have a panicked kid, unprepared, with no tools, potentially in the midst of a horrible situation, alone. Let's not do that to our children.

Similar to my Halloween discussion, parents must have conversations with their kids about smart phones, gaming devices, apps, challenges, and more. Not doing this, and handing them a gadget anyway, is setting them up for failure, and worse—danger. As we become more aware of the real risks and dangers the online world presents, we must develop a plan that will help us manage this ever-changing landscape. Before we launch into our tools, we need to first determine what age our children will get a phone (or more accurately, get access to the online world) and second, determine how to talk to them about the really hard stuff they will face.

WHEN TO ALLOW A PHONE

You may have heard of the national campaign called "Wait Until 8th," which recommends that parents do not give a child a phone until they're in eighth grade nor access to data until they're 16. The reason this program chooses 8th grade is based on research that indicates phones interfere with schoolwork and grades, they are addictive, change one's childhood, increase anxiety and depression, interfere with sleep, and expose children to inappropriate content. While it's a great campaign, unless kid groups are doing it together, it's tough to single out a child and make them wait until 8th grade alone. If you can get the parents of your child's friends to agree, it's truly a great idea. The fact is, most kids are getting a phone around 5th or 6th grade, when they are 10 or 11 years old. But when should your child get a smart phone? That answer depends wholly on their ability to handle the critically important conversations related to having a phone, as well as the rules you will place around their phone ownership.

I have three kids, and while they were all born within a 3.5-year span (all via c-section mind you—sometimes I think my body has still not recovered) and while they are being raised in the exact same household with the same rules, same schools, same parents, they are very different in almost every way. They have matured at different ages; they have different strengths, and they have very different love languages. While I've had critical conversations about the online jungle with each of them based on the guiding principles I've developed, I've done so with these three parameters in mind. Age is an essential factor, and the language used must be age appropriate. That said, maturity counts for more. Depending on maturity, this might bump your conversation up or down a notch. And be honest. Suppose you are giving your child an iPad with access to YouTube Kids or their first gaming device or smartphone. In that case, you must have conversations about the online world in an honest, age-appropriate and maturity-appropriate manner. As we go through the tools and exercises in the next few chapters, I will expound further on this point and provide tips to get you to an answer. Stay with me!

OFFLINE CONVERSATIONS FOR AN ONLINE WORLD

As you navigate whether your tween or teen is ready for a smartphone, you must strategically discuss the issues they may encounter. (Yes, such strategic conversations are outlined all throughout this book.) Remember, teens especially are wired to push away from their parents, so expect a level of pushback. But also know that kids crave their parents' approval more than anything else in the world. They may be pushing back on conversations on the outside, but on the inside, your words are planting seeds in their tender souls.

They want this. Remember, kids thrive with boundaries even though they will push on them. Boundaries say, "I love you. I see you. I want to protect you."

Parents, here are some basic tips before you begin talking to your kids:

- **Have a roadmap of topics you want to talk about.** For example, you'll want to address expectations, trust, time management, online choices, risks, and dangers. I've provided road maps of specific topics throughout this book.

- **Have your own opinions about issues.** Raise your child to know what the family values and family rules are. As they get older, allow them to hear you explore these issues anew. This opens the door for them to talk to you. If they think, "I already know my mom would kill me if I told her I got into a car with Lindsay when I wasn't allowed to," your child will preemptively keep this information from you. That said, train them to see how conversations and expectations change with age. Here is an example of a rule presented to a younger kid: "We don't get into cars with certain people." Here is how the rule might be presented in the teen years (depending on their maturity): "While we should never get in the car with certain people, I can imagine moments when you might be invited to ride with an unapproved driver. I think about what that might be like for you when you are feeling the pressure of the moment. Let's talk about how to handle that." This shift in conversation based on age, maturity, and honesty tells them you are fair, you trust them. These kinds of conversations can really be helpful.

- **Be prepared to hide your expressions.** When they talk, just listen. I also suggest taking private notes while you listen to help you process while maintaining your poker face. (Make two columns. On one side list things that you want to die over, and on the other side list new things that come to mind to discuss.) But listen, let them talk, and then share your responses calmly and with positive purpose.

- **Work to capture their attention.** Be strategic about when and where you have these conversations. Perhaps plan to talk in the car or when both of you have just sat down to eat.

- **Think of and find real-life examples of issues you want them to understand.** If you think they cannot handle the topic, or the real-life story, that's a huge indicator that they are not ready! This is my "Golden Rule" discussed more on the next page.

- **Try to use positive language wherever possible.** Set them up for success. "I know you will make the right decision, but come to me whenever you are in doubt. Know that because I love you, there will be consequences for your actions, but they will be fair and only for your best."

THE GIFT AND CURSE OF TECHNOLOGY

Giving your child a phone as a way to reach you is different than giving them access to social media, streaming, or the online world. Personally, I feel it's vital that a child in today's world always has a way to contact a parent, whether that be through a cell phone, a Gizmo, Gabb Phone, walkie talkie, or something else. The question of giving them global accessibility via online technology, however, is a completely different topic and one we must separate. But keep reading to determine if your child is ready for that type of connectivity.

In Section Two of this book, we'll unpack four tools and dive into really specific content that children will encounter when dealing with the online world. As we uncover those issues, you'll be guided through a discussion with your child. In addition to speaking honestly and factoring in their age and maturity, think about my Golden Rule which is this: As you learn about the issues, if you feel that the conversations around those issues (for example, what your child might see or the type of people they might engage with online) will scare them or make them too uncomfortable, then they are not ready for a gadget or device that connects them to the online world. If they can't handle the conversation in a way that allows them to think through a strategy, they are not ready for action steps on how to respond to difficult issues. Period.

Furthermore, as you talk through the tools in the coming chapters, add in personal family values and expectations, where appropriate. And listen to your child. This conversation strategy is built on listening too. As a parent or caretaker, share why you think what you think. Recognize that in the end, "parents vs kids vs technology" is not a fair fight. They might win every single time depending on their online savviness, so handle this very strategically. Ensure it's a win-win conversation for all of you. Now, having said that, if talking about the realities of the online world is difficult for you as a parent, as long as your child has a device, you must. Getting support from a coparent, spouse, grandparent, or family friend who can read this book with you might be helpful. Believe me, as a parent I know how difficult these realities are, but for sake our children, we must do whatever it takes to prepare them.

Rania's Golden Rule

· ·

If you feel that your child cannot handle the conversations around the issues they will face online, then they are not ready for a gadget or device that connects them to the online world.
Period.

· ·

CHAPTER 5

Apps, Challenges, and Chain Letters...Oh My!

The most dangerous neighborhood for your child to be in is in your own house, online.

**ELEANOR KENNELLY GAETAN, PH.D
VICE PRESIDENT AND DIRECTOR OF PUBLIC POLICY
NATIONAL CENTER ON SEXUAL EXPLOITATION**

We now know that large parts of the entire world are on all the same platforms as our kids. We also know that our children spend more time on these platforms with these people and they are being exposed to more things than ever before. We also know that the average age now for getting a first phone is 10.3 years old.[63] With all these reasons and more, it's the perfect time to stop and create an online plan for your kid—one that they will agree to and that works! To do that, we have to have an idea of what our children are doing online. If you are anything like me or the many parents I speak with daily, this is where we start to feel overwhelmed. We do not know where our kids "are" when they go online or

---

63 (Influence Central, accessed 5-26-20) https://internetsafety101.org/mobilestatistics.

CHAPTER FIVE

what apps they are "hanging out" in. We have no idea what "online challenges" are trending or why they are dangerous. Sure, we remember the chain letters of yesteryear, but we have no idea how that works in the online world and what the risks could be. And we have never stopped to think about the impact of these activities on our children. But we must, and I'm going to break it all down for you. I'm going to turn all this unknown "gray space" into a concrete action plan that you control. I'm going to make this process easy and evergreen. In the coming chapters, I will give you a "tool belt" of safe strategies for your kids, but before we get into the "how," we need to tackle the "what." We need a basic understanding of what kids do online. With countless apps to choose from, I've approached this topic by creating "buckets," or categories of apps, that make up the online world, collectively known as platforms. It's impossible to know every new and developing platform, and because I want us to move into a sustainable way of navigating the online world, we are going to have to shift our view from microscopic to macroscopic, or wide angle. So instead of learning about individual apps, we are going to look at collective categories of apps. Once we identify the categories, or buckets, we will define them, place rules around them, and create an evergreen strategic plan regarding the entire bucket, once and for all. With this approach, your online plan does not live or die based on any specific app or game that may be trending one minute and gone the next; it lasts.

Keep in mind, many platforms will fit into multiple buck-

APPS, CHALLENGES, AND CHAIN LETTERS...OH MY!

ets. For example—some people post on Instagram to show their creativity; others post on Instagram to sell products; still others have Instagram but never post, they just enjoy consuming people's content. That's okay. It will all come together in the end because your rules will be about activities, not so much the individual app. So, let's get started by reviewing the "buckets" list below, then go through the exercise that follows.

PLATFORM/APP "BUCKETS"

While there are nearly two million apps in the app store, I've distilled them down into 16 categories. Over time, others may develop, but this will give you a streamlined approach to establishing rules around what your kids are doing online.

- **Socializing Apps:** The most common include but are not limited to Instagram, SnapChat, Facebook, Facebook Messenger, Kik, WhatsApp, Viber, GroupMe, Discord, MeetMe, and Yubo. This is undoubtedly the largest bucket and typically the first reason a child wants a phone. Users on social platforms are there to hang out and socialize. Often, your popularity on apps like this depends on how many you connect and "socialize" with or engage with (Parents, think about it; how many times have you heard your kids talk about the number of followers they or a friend has?). Users on these platforms thrive when relationships are maintained and large numbers of connections are established. These

CHAPTER FIVE

apps usually allow "in-app" text messaging, face-to-face talking, video sharing, and more. Do you know how to access or read the chat or text message within your child's social media apps?

- **Random Chat Apps:** Examples include Strangers, MeetMe, Monkey, Skout, BeeTalk, Twoo, Hitwe, Flurv, HOLLA Live, Golu, Qeep, CamGo, and Omegle. These apps focus on socializing but do so based on connecting kids with random people—a.k.a. complete strangers—to start a conversation. For users here, it's not about longevity or building relationships but rather accumulating random exchanges.

- **Live Streaming & Video Chat Apps:** Examples include Bigo Live, Houseparty, Periscope, Live.me, YouNow, Marco Polo, Monkey, Omegle, Twitch, HOLLA, and ChatLive. On these devices, kids can talk and see each other via video, in real time. While some platforms do not record, people engaging with you (or your child) can "screen record," so these sessions should never be considered private. These connections can also be random, and anyone video chatting can acquire all kinds of information from your child's setting.

- **Photo and video sharing for the purpose of crafts, art, cooking, organizing, dancing, room décor, digital design and more:** Examples include Pinterest, VSCO, TikTok, Musically, and Look. Most of our kids have talents and interests that they want to spend time reading about and sharing content on. This seems perfectly fine, but guidelines are necessary for all the same reasons as the other apps. There are private chat features in these apps just like all the others, along with GPS tracking, and nefarious platform users who have access to your child.

- **Forum & Discussion Networks:** Examples include Twitter, Parler, Reddit, 4Chan, Amino, and Quora. Some think of these platforms as the "front page" of the internet. These sites can be a great way to keep up on the latest trends, but they can also be home to unfiltered content and often brutal commentary. Foul language, propaganda, hate speech as well as bullying are common on these sites. Content, for the most part, is opinion based and can often be extreme, which draws eyeballs.

- **Platform Used for Microblogging:** Examples include Twitter, Tumblr, Plurk, Gab, Reddit, Micro, Medium, and Twister. These platforms allow you to blog. People constantly share images and thoughts with more of an emphasis placed on thoughts and ideas.

- **Dating Apps:** These apps change often but examples include MeetMe (no age verification), MyLol (users 13-19), Tinder (12-19 average age), Kik (message friends and strangers, free), Skout (lack of safety settings), Hot or Not (accessed via Facebook), Spot a Friend (accessed via Facebook), Yubo (real $ purchases), Bumble, CoffeeMeetsBagels, Grinder, Hinge, and others. Not much explanation needed here, but users on these apps are

CHAPTER FIVE

there to date or simply hook up. **Parents beware:** These apps are made for kids as young as 12 years old if not younger. Beyond that, there is no verification of age before you join the app, so anyone can be on, connecting with anyone of any age.

- **Platforms Used for Cyberbullying:** Yes, there really are platforms that thrive on tearing people down. Let's keep in mind that bullying exists on all platforms where people gather, especially young people, but there are some platforms that allow users to be a bit meaner than other platforms. Ask.fm is one of the most concerning, but don't discount Instagram, Facebook, Twitter, SnapChat, and other monster-sized apps. In fact, SnapChat had an app called YOLO that allowed users to send anonymous messages to each other in the form of answering questions posted to SnapChat. YOLO was suspended after a teen boy committed suicide due to the bullying he endured on the app. Again, bullying exists on all apps.

- **Platform Used for Anonymous Social Networks:** Examples include Qooh.me, Ask.fm, Tellonym, Whisper, and Lipsi. Anonymity is one of the most difficult aspects of the online world. It gives people courage to do and say things they never would face-to-face or if their identity were known. The reality is most youth feel anonymous actions are consequence-free. We have to remind them that is a dangerous position to operate out of. Nothing is ever anonymous. Everything shared online lives forever

APPS, CHALLENGES, AND CHAIN LETTERS...OH MY!

and can eventually be traced back to its original poster.

- **Platform Used for Gaming:** Examples include Fortnite, Call of Duty, Twitch, Roblox, and Xbox live. Kids are able to join networks and play with people around the globe. While this is a fun way to connect with friends, when kids play games with strangers or people they don't know in real life, it opens the door to danger, often, predators will pretend to be kids and play for hours before they start asking children private or personal information. And just as often, as the time passes, kids feel comfortable and don't notice they are sharing personal information. Sometimes kids are asked to join the "private networks" or "private servers" of others. If dealing with strangers online, the answer should be no. Additionally, depending on the game, there's usually the option to chat/text message with the other player.

- **Platform Used for Gaming Chat Groups:** There are apps for gaming and then there are apps for gaming chats. Examples include Discord, Mumble, TeamSpeak, and even Skype. These are really places to socialize, but because of the nature of games in general, (they can be violent, sexual, and contain a lot of bullying aspects), it's important to note that conversations around gaming can be uniquely filled with hate speech, shaming, stereotyping, and a lot of "us" vs "them" language.

- **Apps for Building a Brand and Following for Money:** Examples include LikeToKnowIt, OnlyFans, TikTok,

CHAPTER FIVE

Instagram, and others. These sites help people build a brand, business, or following so they can monetize their likes, talents, interests, and assets. There are many red flags when it comes to this type of activity. Building a brand because a child can sing or make crafts is one thing, but gaining notoriety for producing sexual content is another. And it happens. Sites like OnlyFans make the latter possible for young girls and it's absolutely terrible. That said, for those kids who have a legitimate skill and are wanting to monetize, it's important for parents and caretakers to be aware of the plan and be highly involved with every decision, post, and conversation around the building of the talent.

- **Streaming Apps:** We have talked about how often children find themselves streaming content. Whether your child is on Netflix, YouTube, YouTube Kids, HULU, Amazon Prime or many others, kids can get lost in the amount of time they spend streaming content. Regarding content, I wish there were general rules on ratings that unite all digital streaming devices but that's not the case. Still, you can limit "Mature" ratings, "R" ratings and other ratings, generally speaking. You can also limit general categories (no "horror"). You can also limit access through parent monitoring programs on some of these streaming devices like YouTube and Netflix. However, children will get around these limitations if they want, or they will end up streaming content on a completely different platform.

- **Pornography Apps:** Sadly, there are many different adult or pornographic apps. Parents, we must be as clear as day. In most states, children under 18 are legally not allowed to view pornographic content and they shouldn't. For those above 18, we must remember that pornography is addictive, time consuming, and expensive. It can lead to violence or an unrealistic understanding of sexual intimacy, as well as significant physical and psychological issues for the consumer. That said, "bait" is all over every app to engage curious and vulnerable young viewers.

- **Gambling Apps:** There are a lot of real money gambling apps that are licensed, vetted, and take security and safety seriously. Others are not constructed the same way so users must always beware. In the end, users can lose hundreds and thousands of dollars before other family members are even aware. As apps range from gambling on sports to playing cards to betting at a casino, many might find something of interest. While the minimum legal gambling age varies by state (and often is either 18 or 21), we know that kids as young as 10 years old form addictions to online gambling.

- **Hidden Apps:** Yes, there are apps literally designed to allow kids to hide content from parents. They come packaged in various ways, but traditionally, they look like a calculator (and actually work as a calculator), but when your child enters a password, the app unlocks a secret space where your child can dump content they do not want you to see. To a child this is about privacy, and if it's a place where they are keeping personal thoughts or ideas, I'm okay with that. However, if it's a place to keep secret conversations they've had with someone else, I'm not. To a predator, secrecy creates power. Our kids need to know that anything they are doing in secret will eventually come to light. Additionally, if they are engaged in a conversation or photo sharing with someone asking them to keep the content private, there is a high probability that those actions will be used against them later.

Ok, I'm exhausted, are you? Maybe you didn't know there were so many types of apps out there. The good news is that you don't have to review two million of them. You only have to create usage rules around the categories, and I will help you do just that!

Family rules should be based on "function and purpose," and then you'll never need to focus on specific apps again moving forward! And now for our first exercise.

APPS, CHALLENGES, AND CHAIN LETTERS...OH MY!

Exercise 1:
Family Plan for Apps Usage

Now you will have the chance to set up boundaries around each bucket so that your family has clear and defined parameters about where they can go online. To create rules that will be successful for your family, you must consider who your child is, and their maturity level. Yes, your rules for each bucket will depend on your family values, but they must also be created based on the age and maturity of each child in the home. This means that some family rules might apply to all family members, but some rules will vary for your oldest child who is 16, compared to your youngest child who may be 10. That said, you should do this exercise with each child. Remember, we are developing core rules here that apply no matter what platform they are on—rules that are clearly based on the intent of the space and the activity it creates.

So, let's now go through each bucket and answer the following questions:

1. What are your general thoughts on each of these categories?
2. Are you okay with your child being on these types of apps?
3. Which buckets are an absolute no?

Do you have gray areas for some of the apps? Maybe there are

CHAPTER FIVE

categories that you are okay with your child viewing (possibly the "Apps for Building a Brand or Following" category?) but you do not want him/her creating or sharing content on these apps. Now, let's bring our kids into the conversation (see Tips for Tweens and Younger Users on page 105). What are your child's thoughts on each of the platforms they are on? Are they able to organize them in categories or buckets? What are their favorites? Maybe they love socializing platforms and truly do use them to socialize. Many use creative apps to learn new things. Do they think dating platforms are a form of people-watching? (I don't recommend allowing this.)

The point is, have a conversation with them and get to the root of why they like or dislike certain platforms. By doing this, you're helping them define the platform in their own minds and place it in a category or bucket themselves. As a family, we can remove the focus off a platform that is here today, gone tomorrow. This approach also gives your child a framework of how to approach platforms they may be using that you are totally unaware of. Together, come up with family rules and guidelines for each type of platform. As you come up with these rules, think of the intent of the app, what type of users are on it, and whether it's possible to be a participant but not be an engager on the platform. For example, you might allow your child to game but have a rule that they cannot exchange messages with anyone on the platform. There should also be hard and clear family rules, such as, "You are never allowed on a pornographic platform."

CONSIDER GPS TRACKING

Generally speaking, most apps use your GPS location. You'll see this when you download an app; you'll often be asked if you want to share your location with the app "always," "only while using the app," or "never." Talk about this with your children. For navigation purposes and FindMyiPhone, for example, you always want to be sharing your location. Maybe for a restaurant app (think Starbucks or Dunkin Donuts), you want to share only while using the app so they can help you find a location nearest to you. But for social apps, gaming apps, and any other apps, my recommendation is to never share your location. There is no reason for a child to open his/her location to a pool of people known and unknown to them. Does your child know which apps have GPS tracking? (See page 272 for instructions to how to turn this off.)

CONSIDER AGREEMENTS/PERMISSIONS

Be careful about "agreements" some apps require when you install them. Let's say you upload a photo from your camera roll to an app that edits or alters it. What rights are you handing over when you do this? Some apps will clearly say that once you've uploaded your photo from your mobile device onto their platform, you've granted them permission to access your camera or camera roll. Many of these same apps won't allow you to even use their features until you've handed over this permission.

CHAPTER FIVE

CONSIDER APP RATINGS

All apps are rated. According to the App Store on Apple:

- 4+ means the app contains no objectionable material.

- 9+ contains mild or infrequent occurrences of cartoons, fantasy, or realistic violence, and infrequent or mild mature, suggestive, or horror-themed content.

- 12+ contains infrequent mild language, frequent or intense cartoon, fantasy, realistic violence, infrequent or mild mature or suggestive themes, or simulated gambling.

- 17+ contains frequent and intense offensive language, frequent and intense cartoon, fantasy, realistic violence; frequent and intense mature, horror, and suggestive themes, plus sexual content, nudity, alcohol, tobacco, and drugs.

It's a good idea to define what the rules are based on the buckets/categories or territories a platform presents but also, as a habit, get your kids to know which ratings they are allowed to engage in and which ones they are not. A great exercise is to ask them to share their top five apps with you right now and then check the rating scores together. Are you okay with what you find? Have a plan for new apps. With every new platform your child engages in, they need to mentally determine which bucket it goes in and apply the family rules. They should also know your general rules for in-app texting or chatting, in-app purchases, and what information can be shared before they download an app (for example, are they allowed to give the home address when asked for an address? Are they ever allowed to share personal information about the school they attend or grade level?). As you work together to define the parameters of usage in a way that makes sense for your child's safety, they will no longer fear losing out on the things they love to do, but they will understand the wisdom in the plan you are creating to keep them healthy and safe.

TIPS FOR TWEENS AND YOUNGER USERS:

If your child is on the younger side and some of this is beyond their maturity level, there's another way to deal with this area; create general rules based on a few characteristics most platforms have. Most apps have GPS tracking. Does your child know what that means? Of the apps they currently use, do they know which have it? What is your family rule on GPS tracking with platforms? What about text, video messaging, FaceTiming, and content sharing? Almost every single app has this. What are your family rules for texting vs video messaging or FaceTiming vs content sharing? Do both you and your child know how a predator or ill-intent person might wish to access you through the platforms your child is on? (You will. Keep reading.) They might befriend you, follow you, and try to engage via chat or FaceTime.

Ultimately, whatever tools the platform uses, predators will try to take advantage of them. We will discuss this more in depth moving forward, but knowing this and discussing how your child should handle requests and conversations from people they do not know will go a long way. Also, ask older siblings to model responsible online habits—and parents, please do the same!

WHAT ABOUT CHALLENGES AND CHAIN LETTERS?

As if you don't have enough to think about, beyond the many apps our kids download and engage with, we also must think about online "challenges" and chain letters and the ramifications of participating in these. The goal here again is to move away from a micro approach to a macro approach. Instead of reviewing each one individually, let's instead create a strategy around the issues generally.

Challenges are very common. You may remember the ALS ice bucket challenge that was designed to raise awareness. But like everything else, things are different now. Today's challenges present a "dare" or "task" to a child who, remember, does not have the advantage of a fully developed prefrontal cortex and will continually choose risk/reward over pause and caution. If a child does a challenge and posts it with success, it's a great "win" for them. But to find traction in the online world, they will look for challenges, dares, or tasks that are more dangerous, gross, or outrageous to participate and share.

It's important for parents to:

- Know these exist
- Talk to your child
- Create family rules around them

Similarly, the chain letters of yesteryear still exist, but they have evolved and are all online. And just like we used to, today's young mind really does stop to think, "What will happen to me if I break this chain?" Real concern exists. Similarly, the promise of something powerful, or good—or of a deep wish being granted when they comply—is sometimes (often) too hard for a developing mind to pass up.

And let's add this fun fact: A lot of these chains contain links with malware or even spyware in them. Children should never click on strange links and enter personal information as part of signing or sharing a chain letter!

Exercise 2:
Family Discussion Around Challenges and Chain Letters

Following are a list of popular online challenges. Go through the list of these challenges with your child and ask them:

1. Have they heard of it?

2. What do they think of it?
3. Do they know anyone who has participated in it?
4. Can they show you a funny or scary or silly challenge that is similar?
5. What are their thoughts about participating?

It's essential to look at the challenge, point out any potential dangers, and identify any parts that seem ridiculous or nonsensical.

So, let's go through them now.

FUNNY CHALLENGES (Usually Not Dangerous):

- **Try Not to Laugh Challenge:** Popularized by YouTubers like Markiplier, this trend involves watching short, funny videos and trying not to laugh. It's simple and harmless, though there's often a lot of laughing at others' expense.

- **Whisper Challenge:** You may have seen this one on Jimmy Fallon. One person wears headphones playing loud music. The other person says a phrase out loud, and the one listening to music tries to read their lips and repeat the phrase. Hilarity ensues.

- **Mannequin Challenge:** A group of people gets together, poses, and freezes in place, and someone with a camera walks around recording the scene while music plays. Even celebrities have gotten in on this one, including

Michelle Obama, Ellen, and Adele.

FOOD CHALLENGES (Can be Dangerous):

- **Eat It or Wear It Challenge**—this one takes some prep. Put some different foods in separate bags and number them. A player chooses a number, checks out the food, and decides to eat it or wear it. If they eat it, they can dump the remainder on another player's head. If they choose to wear it, you can guess what happens. This challenge is low risk, other than a huge mess (and food allergies).

- **Hot Pepper Challenge**—you can probably guess. Eat a super hot pepper, like a habanero or a ghost pepper, while you film yourself suffering and chugging milk to try to stop the burning. Though most people get through it unscathed, there have been a few reports of people ending up at the hospital.

- **Cinnamon Challenge**—eat a spoonful of cinnamon, sputter and choke, and record the whole thing for others to enjoy. Again, though there may be some temporary discomfort, most kids won't get hurt—but some have.

PHYSICAL CHALLENGES (Can be Dangerous):

- **Backpack Challenge:** This one's a little like running a gauntlet. One person runs between two rows of people who try to hit you with heavy backpacks. The goal is to make it to the end without falling down, but no one ever does. Of course, it's easy for kids to get hurt doing this.

- **Kylie Lip Challenge:** Oh, Kylie Jenner and her lips. In an effort to replicate them, kids would put a shot glass over their mouths, suck in, and make their lips swell artificially. Not only can it cause damage, but it also can be an indicator of body insecurities and the emulation of impossible beauty standards.

DANGEROUS CHALLENGES (Definitely Dangerous):

- **Devious Licks Challenge:** This challenge asks students to destroy school property and post the video. It's recently changed to include assaulting teachers or others in the school as part of the viral video making. Many students have actually been arrested and charged for this type of activity, and TikTok (the main platform where it originated) has promised to ban the videos.

- **Choking/Fainting/Pass-Out Challenge:** To get a high or faint, kids either choke other kids, press hard on their chests, or hyperventilate. Obviously, this is very risky, and has resulted in death.

- **Tide Pod Challenge:** Biting into a pod of laundry detergent is clearly not a good idea, but kids are doing it and posting videos of the results. Because the outside coating of the pods is meant to dissolve, they release their contents into a kid's mouth very quickly and cause chemical burns and kidney and lung problems.

- **Blue Whale Challenge:** Though some challenges are physically dangerous, this one truly frightens parents. Over the course of 50 days, an anonymous "administrator" assigns self-harm tasks, like cutting, until the 50th day, when the participant is supposed to commit suicide. It is rumored to have begun in Russia. There are reports that suicides were tied to this challenge, but those are unverified and likely not true. Apps related to the Blue Whale Challenge were said to appear and were then removed. The biggest concern is teens who are at risk and may be susceptible to trends and media about suicide, because even if the challenge began as an isolated incident or hoax, it could become real.

- **Squid Games Challenge or Honeycomb Challenge:** In which participants try to create a thin sheet of honeycomb and then carve out a shape using only a pin. The thin candy cannot be broken. The problem is, kids, some as young as 6, are getting severely hurt or burned trying to make the sugar base.

- **Run the Gauntlet Challenge:** Participants go to specific sites and watch extremely horrific videos back-to-back until you get to the end of the series of videos with each video being far worse than the last. The idea is that if you can make it through all the videos, you are essentially desensitized to anything on the internet. Within seconds, kids access the most vile, horrific content that humanity has to offer, which can in fact deeply emotionally damage them.

WHY THIS MATTERS

If you're thinking to yourself that this might be a mundane exercise for super sharp kids, remember that most kids get a cell phone in late elementary school. We need to start these conversations when they are young. Also remember that children need to understand the nuances of the landscape they are traveling to ensure that they don't trip over the "lure" of anything negative. We also want to ensure that these conversions grow with them, wherever they find themselves online.

And finally, let's never underestimate the power of the masses. When millions find a dare, task, or challenge funny or fascinating, it will quickly pull others in, even those who you think would never be interested. Let's face it, most of us would stop to watch these videos. Children choose to stop and add content.

WANT TO THROW TECHNOLOGY OUT THE WINDOW?

Some parents reading this might want to throw technology out the window and be done with it. Believe me, I do! But we can't. It's the way we all communicate—especially our kids. The current language of socializing amongst youth is via online communication—apps, social media, texting, DMs, gaming, followers, and more—it's their reality. As I said earlier, in my opinion, it's hard to forbid a child in today's world from engaging online. But that's why we are doing the critically important work to spend time building an evergreen tool belt built on a foundation of protection.

And remember, parents, our kids have a myriad of ways to access the online world:

- Their smartphone
- Your smartphone
- Tablets—I can't tell you how many parents I talk to who say, "Oh, I'm not getting little Bobby a cell phone until he's 14" but little Bobby has had an iPad with full access to the internet and streaming platforms, gaming apps, etc. since he was eight.
- Kindle
- Their computer
- Your computer
- Friends' electronics

CHAPTER FIVE

- School electronics

And let's not forget that even if you've forbidden them from having apps, many still have the accounts. Parents, I've talked to so many kids who delete their Instagram app each morning to pass a "parent check" but either reinstall the app the second they get back the phone or just go to www.instagram.com to view and manage their accounts. Sure, these parents check screen time and look at search histories, but kids today know how to get around all of that.

PARENT HACK: There is one place on a phone that tracks where the user has been and the amount of time they've spent on each app that cannot be altered. This magical source of information is found in the "battery usage" section of the phone, and it's simple to check:

- **iPhone**—visit SETTINGS → BATTERY and wait for the information to load. You'll see a child's screen time and how much time they've spent on various apps. It will show time over the last 24 hours and the last 10 days. Here's an actual screenshot from my phone right now.

- **Android**—visit SETTINGS → BATTERY and tap the three-dot menu at the top-right. From the menu that appears, hit "Battery Usage." You'll be taken to a screen that shows you a list of apps that have consumed your battery since its last full charge. For a complete list of details, tap the three-dot menu button at the top-right again and select "Show full device usage" to view information from system processes like the operating system itself.

As much as kids try, they cannot manipulate this information. It will clearly show you what app a child has been using as well as how much time they've spent.

Android System Settings — iPhone System Settings

THE GOOD NEWS

In a culture that's become extremely "cause" focused, there's a lot of good that young minds can tap into online. Encourage kids to follow charitable work where you live, in

CHAPTER FIVE

your state, and around the globe. Let's engage in positive online challenges and help good things go viral! And guess what? Kids who follow more positive online engagement find themselves personally less anxious and cultivate a more authentic engagement, and that's a win-win for everyone.

Ok parents, great job taking apps, challenges, and chain letters to task. You've gotten your feet wet with the idea of having deeper conversations with your kids, and I understand that for some families, this alone can be a challenge. But keep at it. Next, we will dive in to my four power tools for keeping kids as safe as possible online.

SECTION TWO

THE FOUR POWER TOOLS

CHAPTER 6

Tool 1: Define Your Online Brand

"Every interaction, in any form, is branding."
SETH GODIN, AUTHOR, TEACHER, ENTREPRENEUR

Now we are getting into my favorite part of the book, and I'm sure it will be yours too—the four "power tools." These are solutions coming from my countless hours of research and experience in this industry since 2006, when I began working for Crime Stoppers. Over the years, I have been actively studying youth and anything that creates danger in their lives. By far, my greatest area of focus has been the subject matter of this book—the nexus between youth development, their engagement in the online world, inherent risks, the role parents play, the lack of understanding parents might have, and the exploration of strategic and evergreen solutions. Suffice it to say, the next few chapters come from many (many, many) hours of researching, conversations, presentations, trial and error, and good ol' fashion sweat and tears. What I've discovered in all of my research is that there are four main areas of online engagement that make our children vulnerable. If we can empower our kids with knowledge and strategy in these four areas of engagement, we can address all the areas of concern in the online world. Best of all, the solutions I'm about to share with you will stand over time, regardless of how the landscape of the online world changes, or a parent's level of understanding about it all. The four areas that my four power tools address are purpose, community, engagement, and posting.

The four power tools will do the following:

- Guide you and your child through a real discussion about the underlying reasons why they are online and define how they want to present themselves to the online community. This is an important foundational piece for all their online engagement.

- Help your child understand who is in their online community, as well as the online community they are not seeing but very much interacting with.

- Help your child be aware of the internal and external threats of being online and develop and exit strategy for when they encounter something potentially harmful.

- Give them a real understanding of the ramifications of engagement, so they can be prepared to face whatever threats come their way.

- Encourage them to always, and at all times, post safely— to know what that means, and give them a framework they will want to follow.

Now, as you go through the four power tools, there will be questions and exercises for you to do with your child. I want to encourage you to first read all the way through the tools so that you have a good understanding of how they all fit together. Then go back and take your time to go through each tool and answer the questions as a family.

Are you ready? Let's dig in...

TOOL 1: DEFINE YOUR CHILD'S ONLINE BRAND

Ok parents, I know I just lost half of you. But stick with me for a second. I'm not at all suggesting that your child is a product or commodity, but let's consider the true definition of a brand. In marketing, your brand, in simple terms, boils down to the image you have, as well as the impression you leave with people in the marketplace. We all have a brand, so to speak, because we all leave an impression with people. But to "add some color" to the idea, here is what some top entrepreneurs have to say about brand:

> *"Your brand is what other people say about you when you're not in the room."*

–Jeff Bezos, founder and executive chairman of Amazon

CHAPTER SIX

> *"Brand is just a perception, and perception will match reality over time."*
>
> —Elon Musk, founder, CEO and chief engineer at SpaceX; Technoking of Tesla

> *"Every interaction, in any form, is branding."*
>
> —Seth Godin, author, teacher, entrepreneur

> *"Your brand expresses the value you provide. It's you."*
>
> —Amy Locurto, founder of livinglocurto.com and iheartfaces.com

Whether we realize it or not, each of us is continually either reinforcing or redefining our brands with every choice we make. I've worked in media and marketing for a long time, and companies understand the importance of branding and go to great lengths to define and protect their brands. I have seen the many guiding questions companies ask. Is the brand clear? What is it always portraying? Will all associations with the brand support the brand image and attract the ideal customer? Some larger companies will spend millions of dollars determining their logo, which is the graphic image that represents who they are, and the language, motto, taglines, and imagery that is part of their brand, asking, "What impression does this leave?" The marketing agency will put together a three-inch binder of "brand guidelines" detailing how the logo can and can't be used in different mediums. They also focus on affiliations and how those might help or hurt the brand. As a company decides how to position their product in the marketplace, it will always be against a backdrop of whether the positioning or associations support the image, the brand, they are trying to portray.

For example, Lexus, a high-end luxury car brand has never deviated from its luxury messaging associates itself with high-end arts, such as the ballet, because the arts align with its brand. Nike keeps a tight hold on inspirational and motivational language, sponsoring sporting events and athletes because that feeds their target audience. Athletes ally themselves with empowering brands because that aligns with their personal desire to empower. Celebrities are no different, and while they are "people, not products" they have entire teams constantly hovering over their image, content, and potential associations and partnerships. Why do companies, athletes, and celebrities do this? Because they understand that people form opinions based on what you put out into the world. They know that to build longevity in the marketplace, you need to astutely and continually think about your image—your brand—and fiercely protect it. They also know the importance of creating a tightrope of guidelines so they do not make a misstep. If you are not diligent about protecting your brand, it places your company and fame (or persona) at risk.

The same type of thinking is true for your child. The wrong messaging could create the wrong brand—the wrong

CHAPTER SIX

impression of your child—and that could place your child at risk. At risk for what? At risk of losing friends, followers, and potential opportunities in the future. They are also at risk of luring the wrong connections and even predators (which I will expand on shortly). So, each of us must build our brands thoughtfully and protect our brands fiercely. And we must do this navigating "real time" changes in culture, language, and opinion. The smartest people do this wisely, without others even knowing it. In a nutshell, your brand is a summary statement defining who you are and what you stand for. Protecting that is extremely important.

"But my child is neither a company nor a celebrity."

Yes and no—and actually, I'll ask you to hold that thought as you consider that the online world is very different from the real world. In the online world, a "celebrity" is someone who has influence and followers. Some kids are pursuing the status of becoming an online influencer (celebrity) while others are simply there to have fun and socialize or to become popular among their peers.

Either way, understanding that we are all online brands gives a clear picture of the importance of one's "voice" and what they post and how they interact with others. It enables us to turn all the gray intangibles of online interacting: commenting, sharing, streaming, content creating, and more, into defined spaces where concrete action steps and guiding principles go with them anywhere they go online—even when mom or dad are not "following" them. And guess what, our kids inherently understand the impact of what I'm saying here even though they have not stopped to think about how it relates to them personally.

I recently asked 100 kids (ages 12–25) via an Instagram survey four questions. The results are very telling:

1. Does what you Post on social define who you are?

    - 49% responded "Yes, it's a reflection."
    - **51% responded "No, post whatever." (majority answer)**

2. Does what you Like on social define who you are?

    - 39% responded "Yes."
    - **61% responded "Don't think about it." (majority answer)**

3. Does what you comment on define who you are?

    - 49% responded "Yes, absolutely!"
    - **51% responded "Don't think about it." (majority answer)**

CHAPTER SIX

But here's the kicker…then I asked:

4. Have you formed opinions of people you don't know based simply on what they post (i.e., they are nice, mean, funny, luxurious, have a great life, promiscuous person or other opinions)?

  - **67% "Yes."**
    (majority answer)
  - 33% "Not really."

Kid's inherently form opinions of others and define others by their posts, likes, and comments—all of which create an online image or brand—even though they fail to realize the same applies to themselves. And because they fail to make the personal connection, they tend to post "whatever." This is what we need to address and change. The fact is that a majority of your child's interactions might be with people they literally do not know, and all of this can and will impact their future. Colleges, employers, camp counselors, internships, or anyone who wants to know about your child will search them online and form opinions of them in the same way your child forms opinions of others based on their posts. And we know very well that these opinions last a lifetime and can have very serious ramifications down the line.

Let's take a modern-day example of someone you have probably heard of—Chrissy Teigen. Chrissy is married to John

Legend. She is a well-loved model, TV host, entertainer, and celebrity chef with millions of followers on Instagram and Twitter. People have flocked to her page for years, drawn to her sharp tongue and banter. But the tide turned when people started digging into her past posts, dating as far back as 10 years, determining that Chrissy was actually more of a bully. This created a firestorm on social media and placed her entire brand in jeopardy. In response, Teigen took to Twitter to write[64]:

> *May 12*
>
> *Not a lot of people are lucky enough to be held accountable for all their past bullshit in front of the entire world. I'm mortified and sad at who I used to be. I was an insecure, attention seeking troll. I am ashamed and completely embarrassed at my behavior but that is nothing compared to how I made Courtney {the target} feel. I have worked so hard to give you guys joy and be beloved and the feeling of letting you down is nearly unbearable, truly. These were not my only mistakes and surely won't be my last as hard as I try but god I will try!!*
>
> *I have tried to connect with Courtney privately but since I publicly fueled all this, I want to also publicly apologize. I'm so sorry, Courtney. I hope you can heal now knowing how deeply sorry I am. And I am so sorry I let you guys down. I will forever work on being better*

---

64 https://twitter.com/chrissyteigen

CHAPTER SIX

than I was 10 years ago, one year ago, six months ago.

In the offline world, or what we know as the "real world," comments disappear almost immediately. People move on. Onlookers don't engage too much with the "he said/she said" scenarios. But online, everything you post lasts a lifetime and beyond. Record is kept of everything you post, everything you search, and everything you click. Even if you delete a post, it can still show up in others' feeds, and it can still live on with a person who took a screenshot of it. Anything posted online has a lifetime of longevity. (Yes, I'm going to keep saying it over and over.)

Here's the deal, Chrissy Teigen is famous and highly influential. She's married to a literal legend (pun intended). But even she couldn't survive the power of old tweets and how they hurt her brand. She lost a lot of respect and a lot of fans. Some might argue that she was not protective of her brand. Others might argue that she simply felt "above it all." For 10 years, it wasn't a problem, and then one day it was, and there's no going back.

It's not just about losing fans and followers. There's also the story of Alexi McCammond, *Conde´ Nast* and *Teen Vogue* editor who was reportedly forced to resign after some decade-old racist tweets resurfaced. McCammond resigned just two weeks after the company had appointed her to her dream position. In her Twitter statement, she said, "Past tweets have overshadowed the work I've done to highlight the people and issues I care about."

The tweets were written in 2011 when McCammond was a teenager. Teenagers say and do things that aren't always characteristic of them, as we all know. But that doesn't matter in the online world. If she had just defined her brand as a young online user and defined it with intention even back then, aware of the long-term effects and consequences, maybe she wouldn't have ever posted the way she did.[65]

Beyond losing business deals and jobs, college students are being kicked out of school and expelled across the country for the same reasons. Most recently, a Georgia college expelled a student who used racial slurs on social media citing "such views have no place on our campus or within our community and we will act decisively when confronted by them."[66] Don't let this happen to your child. This first "tool" is all about thinking ahead and being aware of the impact of your actions.

BRINGING IT HOME: LET'S TALK ABOUT IT!

These stories are sobering and hopefully thought-provoking. Now, it's time to bring all of this home—to your home. Following are some questions you can discuss with your kids to help them understand and define their brand and bring awareness to the importance of every online interaction. We'll get a little more granular about this topic in just a bit, but for now start with a conversation. Before you have this

---

[65] https://twitter.com/alexi/status/1372603793825751040?s=20 https://www.nytimes.com/2021/03/18/business/media/teen-vogue-editor-alexi-mccammond.html
[66] https://www.nbcnews.com/news/us-news/georgia-college-student-who-used-racial-slur-social-media-post-n1225936

discussion, read the stories in this chapter with them. Carefully choose a time when you and your tween/teen can have good communication. For example, some kids are too tired after school or sports for these types of conversations and do better around the dinner table or before bedtime.

Exercise 3:
Family Brand Discussion

1. Who are your favorite online influencers? Is there someone online (known in real life or whom you just follow) that you used to admire but then found out was a total fraud? What happened to them? How was the rise and fall? How quick was it? What did you personally think about that person before and after?

2. When you post online, are you thinking about what other people will think about you?

    a. If the answer is Yes: Do you post because you want to say something? Do you post because you want people to like you? Or do you post to get likes?

    b. When you like someone else's post online, do you think that what you've liked reflects who you are?

3. When you share someone else's post online, do you think what you've shared reflects who you are?

DEFINE YOUR ONLINE BRAND

4. When you comment on someone else's post online, do you think what you've shared reflects who you are?

5. Do you form opinions of other people based on what they post, like, or share?

6. What opinions do you form when someone posts something? Choose as many as you like:

   a. A kind post means a kind person posted it.

   b. A mean post means a mean person posted it.

   c. A funny post means a funny person posted it.

   d. I think most people are playing a role online and what they post is not their true selves.

   e. I don't care what they post but I look at how they treat others online.

   f. A post can make you look shallow.

   g. I form opinions of people based on what they post.

   h. I don't think I post enough for people to form opinions of me.

   i. Something else

7. What opinions do you form when someone likes something? Choose as many as you like:

   a. Liking a kind post means you are a kind person.

    b. Liking a mean post means you are a mean person.

    c. Liking a funny post means you have a sense of humor.

    d. I think most people like posts to just be liked by the person posting.

    e. I think most people are playing a role online and what they like is not really showing their true selves.

    f. I don't care what they like but do care what they post.

    g. Something else

8. What opinions do you form when someone shares something? Choose as many as you like:

    a. Sharing a kind post means you are a kind person.

    b. Sharing a mean post means you are a mean person.

    c. Sharing a funny post means you have a sense of humor.

    d. I think most people share posts to just be liked by the person posting.

    e. I think most people are playing a role online and what they share is not really showing their true selves.

    f. I don't care what they share but I do care what they

post.

    g. I don't care what they share but I do care what they like.

    h. I don't think I share enough posts for people to form opinions of me

    i. Something else

9. Which of the following most influences your opinions of others online?

    a. Number of followers

    b. How they behave online

    c. What they look like

    d. Perceived lifestyle/experiences

    e. Their friend circle

    f. Fame

10. Do you think it's fair to say that you form opinions of others based purely on what they like?

11. Could you say that you like or don't like someone based on his or her online personality?

12. Have you gone from liking to not liking someone based completely on what they've posted, liked, commented, or shared?

13. Do you think it's possible to lose a job or a chance to go to a certain school based on what you post online?

    a. Have you ever heard of this happening to anyone you know?

    b. Do you know what a brand is? If so, what is it?

    c. Can a person be a brand? If so, how?

15. Before you post, do you stop and think: Is this something I would say or do face-to-face? Would I be okay with this photo/quote of mine being posted in the school hallways?

Now, let's ask the kids about us, the parents. These are vital questions to ask them to answer honestly. Please don't get mad at their answers. Praise honesty while working through shocking moments!

1. What do your parents think about your social media usage?

2. Do your parents really know what you are posting?

3. Do they know why you are on social media?

4. Do they have access to your accounts?

5. Have your parents talked to you about online safety?

6. Do you like their posts?

7. Are you ever embarrassed by what they share?

What we post, like, share, and comment on stays with us and defines us (and that's okay!). That's why our very first tool in our toolbox begins here. Parents, let's start by helping our children zero in on what their brand is as well as what they/you want it to be.

"DEFINE YOUR BRAND" ACTION PLAN

Following is a list of starter questions that will help create a foundation for your child's brand and overall online strategic plan. Remember parents, we are not telling our kids NOT to post or engage online, but rather we want them to know why they are online, what they hope to achieve with their online engagement, and how to behave online with an understanding of the impact. Answering these simple questions will create a lasting road map of what's right for them and for your family.

As you ask these questions, let your child be honest, please! Don't try to shape their answer to what you want, but let it come from their heart. If your child looks at you and says, "All I want to do is be famous and go viral," that is an absolute win even if that's not what you want, and you'll see why as we move on. Inviting you into that process and allowing for your guidance, will help them navigate the online world more safely. If you disapprove of their ultimate goals, at least stop to celebrate the realization of what those goals actually are and then discuss your concerns together in a way that begins with being on the same page. In that case, having an honest conversation, thinking through what it means to be famous or go viral (for example) might enlighten them to the fact that it might not really be what's best for them. And guess what—this might be the first time they've said this out loud and had a chance to think it all through! Or it might be the beginning of an opportunity for them to go after something and see what happens.

The most important thing in all of this is having honest, open conversations. We want to help our kids share openly with us, to take control of shaping their online identity and start thinking about their posts so they are no longer posting in a lazy, non-strategic manner. And parents, your kids will likely change their minds over time anyway. They are, after all, just kids. And because they will likely change their minds over time, I suggest scheduling this conversation as a yearly "check in" to make sure you stay on the same page.

Exercise 4:
Brand Development Starter Questions

The following brand starter questions are to give you and your child something to think about as you read through the next section. Don't worry if your child can't answer these questions immediately. It takes time to develop a brand and the following guidance will help!

DEFINE YOUR ONLINE BRAND

1. Why is your child online? (They may not immediately be able to answer this. See the next section.)
2. Do they recognize that they have a brand or an image? Do they realize that they are a brand no matter where they are online and what they post, share, like, or comment? (Remember, this is not bad—it's just an important understanding to navigate a clear plan forward.)
3. What do they think their brand is currently?
4. Parents, what do you think their brand is currently?
5. If they could dream up a brand that reflects them, what would it be?
6. What needs to change?

START WITH "WHY"

So, why is your child really online? This is one of the most important questions you'll ask. In any arena, we have to start with "why" because "why" shapes everything else—who, what, when, where, and how. We must know why our children are online and what they are hoping to achieve online before we can help them solidify their brand and where it needs to go.

CHAPTER SIX

Let's dig deeper into that first question.

Is your child online to:

- Be seen?
- Be consumed?
- Become famous?
- Make money/endorse or sell products?
- Create products?
- Develop relationships? What kind? This is important Some kids revel in the social/antisocial reality of online socializing. They can keep in touch with others without having to go out. Others are trying to build an army of friends or seek special relationships. The point is, have you ever asked your child these questions? Now is the time.
- Simply be social?
- Connect with as many people as possible?
- Troll others?
- Show love?
- Show hate?
- Be popular?
- Pass time?
- Share their emotions/creativity?

- Help engage when they are really introverts?

There may be many answers to this question, and the answers may change many times, but please do this exercise and do it every few months to check on your kids and where their online lives are going. Once you know why they are online, you can start defining what their brand should be. Those two factors will lay the groundwork for everything else.

Example 1: "I want to be famous" or "I want to be seen."

A sit down with 333 kids between the ages of nine and 15 showed the following:

- 80% owned cell phones
- 100% went online daily
- 100% regularly watched TV and YouTube
- Shockingly, 40% ranked "fame" first in a list of seven values (community feeling, image, benevolence/kindness, fame, self-acceptance, financial success, and achievement).[67]

And let's face it, a kid seeking fame online is not an anomaly. Many kids want to be online famous. A child who wants to be "famous" (a celebrity or influencer) or to be "seen" as popular with a lot of followers, will need to intentionally build a following that will rely on their consistent brand.[68]

---

67 https://www.greatschools.org/gk/
68 Parents, as I write this, I'm coming from the perspective of the child's safety only.

CHAPTER SIX

This child will most likely have a public account, be followed by people unknown to all of you, and will encounter things online that are not age appropriate. All these things will be discussed in the other three tools, but right now, our focus is having honest conversations that help kids do what they're going to do in the safest way possible. (As long as it's age appropriate and legal, of course!) For the child who wants to be famous, recognizing that they are a brand, defining what that brand is, and understanding that they must stay true to their brand is key. They also need to know that others who don't know them in real life will form opinions based solely on what they post, like, comment, and share. They must curate their posts accordingly, as this will be necessary for success and safety. I'm not saying they cannot be creative, silly, funny, or random, but I am saying that once you step back to understand their goals and the longevity of their engagement, you can help them post even silly and random things strategically and safety. For example, a child who has a goal of being "famous" or "seen" might want to post randomly from her dorm room. That is okay, but she must do so strategically, never sharing what building she is in or what floor, or her dorm room number. Why? Because this child has defined her path, she knows and understands that to get there, she's allowing for many followers, most unknown to her. She should never share information that a stranger can

---

While I'll be talking about how to build a consistent brand, what I'm really trying to do is create a tight rope for our kids to hold onto, using terms and a concept they understand. The concept of homing in on a brand and defining it with you will truly help keep them from making grave errors online, now and down the road.

use to find her current location. She must post with intention and safety always in the forefront of her mind.

Defining some of these things will also keep them from going all over the place or falling victim to trends or dangerous challenges in the hopes of "going viral." It can keep them from doing random stunts that can ultimately hurt the brand they are building. The goal is to work with our kids to build a strategic foundation, with an abundance of direction from you.

Please also know that I don't judge or criticize kids who seek fame or popularity. I just want them to also understand the ramifications. To be a celebrity or open your life to be seen by all, means you're striving for the "attention" of the masses. It means you're opening your world to a wide variety of people. What you post will have value to many, but in addition to accolades and free goodies, you're also opening yourself up to getting scrutinized and judged, constantly. Your audience will absorb everything you say or do, and that can be a lot of pressure. Is that something you really want for your child? Does your child really want that for him/herself?

Example 2: "I want to connect with friends."

Some kids may be more private and only want to use social media to engage with friends. That's great. In this case, considering most of their community will be people known to them, their "brand" is going to be made up of both their in-person persona which is complimented, or

CHAPTER SIX

hurt, by their online brand. Their online engagement is still critically important but for different reasons than in example #1. This child needs to focus on consistency. For example, are they kind in person but a bully online? They also must remember that content from even private accounts can be seen by the masses and eventually, everything and anything they post has the potential to be seen by all. Even if they are in a closed online circle surrounded by true friends, content shared must still match their real personal brand and stand the test of time. These are only two different examples of why someone is online. You and your family will take the time to answer this question for yourselves. When the "why" is clear, when you know what the goal is, everything else becomes clear as well.

So, now that you know why, let's decide on what the brand will be: At this point, it's important to discuss the value of authenticity in defining your child's brand. It's easy to hide behind an online persona where people can be someone other than who they really are. It may be easy, but it's not healthy. Your child's brand should reflect who they truly are–their values and convictions. Even if they think it's harmless to pretend to be someone or something they aren't, invariably the truth will come out. Just ask Hilaria Baldwin. Hilaria Baldwin is a mom and influencer married to actor Alec Baldwin (Hailey Bieber's uncle) who lost her credibility when it was discovered that the brand she was portraying was not true to her real persona. Born "Hillary Thomas" to white

American parents in Boston, Hillary married famous actor Alec Baldwin in 2012. Some say she used the famous name to push her interests in health and lifestyle into the spotlight. In doing so, she presented herself as "Hilaria," a native of Spain whose native language was Spanish. In 2020, it was discovered that Hilaria was in reality a native New Englander and the online world lost their minds. She lost business deals with American Girl and the baby label Cuties Baby Care. She lost followers and her standing in the influencer community. And it's all because she misrepresented herself and built a brand around that misrepresentation. What's really interesting is that Hilaria, or Hillary, never specifically said she was one thing or another. She just consistently presented herself in a certain way. People formed strong opinions and she let them. But when the misrepresentation was discovered, people poured over every post she ever made. In fact, the online website *INSIDER* shared this. "*INSIDER* went through Baldwin's Instagram-post history, her tweets, her family's blog posts, and seven years' worth of public interviews to see how her statements on her background have evolved since she married and joined the public spotlight."[69] Can you imagine? They went through *seven* years of her posts and interviews just to "catch" her! So rather than go through all that, decide now if are you posting as yourself or as a character, and then make it clear to your audience and be consistent. This is what YouTuber Miranda Sings has done

---

69 https://www.insider.com/hilaria-baldwin-spanish-controversy-public-life-timeline-2020-12

so well. She created a persona, but her following knows it and loves it. If you are posting as you, remember, people value authenticity above all else, especially in a virtual world. If you are posting as a character (which can and should evolve overtime), make it clear to your followers.

BRAND REVIEW

A business brand summarizes the characteristics, thoughts, actions, intent, purpose and agenda of a product or person in the business world. The best brands are consistent and develop audiences or followers who want to identify with them and trust they will continually represent themselves along with their brand guidelines. In the case of a child who desires to be famous, they should similarly painstakingly think about how they define their brand. They should be strategic and not fall victim to online trends, social media challenges, or viral whims that take them off brand or off message. Remember, they can delete their posts, but their followers (again, a majority of whom they do not know) will save, share, and screenshot their posts, and will love or hate them on a dime. A child who wishes to be famous or become an influencer must treat his/her brand no differently than a business brand. Even kids without business or celebrity goals are brands. They are personal brands. Personal brands are supported by who you are in person. Followers tend to be a little bit more lenient with slight variations of your brand. They will for sure, call you out and let you know when they don't like your online actions, so be prepared!

Please note: Once this is ingrained and understood, a child will know that it doesn't matter what platform they are on or whether or not you are physically monitoring them. They will have a desire to stay true to the brand they've developed and react appropriately wherever they are online. We know it's impossible to keep up with every platform. So let's train our kids how to handle themselves instead by making sure every post, comment, like, and engagement has brand consistency.

Exercise 5:
Brand Refinement

Now that we've explored the idea of a brand and why your child is online, we have some more questions to think about to really shape and refine your child's brand.

Here are some important considerations to ask your child about their brand:

1. What do you want to communicate about yourself to your community? What do you want people to say about you when you're not around?

2. What values do you and your family hold as important? (Respect, honesty, faith, loyalty, integrity, etc.) Does your "why" align with your family values? What about your school's moral code of conduct? Example:

CHAPTER SIX

There are minors gaining fame by posting sexually inappropriate content on OnlyFans.

3. What issues are important to you?
4. What problems are important to you that you can influence and help solve?
5. How do you want people to feel when they've viewed your profile or read your posts?
6. Does your online life contradict your real life anywhere?

Now, let's consider how the way you post impacts your brand:

7. Will you like everything and follows everyone? What does that say about you?
8. Will you be bold and stand up for others and not like, comment on, or share, anything negative?
9. Will you have an account but not post? Or will you post continually? What's your focus and goal with your posting?
10. Will you emote online and post when you are in a heightened emotional state? What does this say about you?
11. What impact does your "why" and your brand have on your future? Consider colleges, graduate schools, future jobs, and future relationships.

In all cases, remember, *exclusivity is a strategy!* The most expensive products in the world are the most exclusive. They are rare—hard to get. The most famous people in the world pick their alliances very carefully. When you create a more "select" brand for yourself, regardless of why you are online (to be seen/famous or to just socialize), it communicates value, and valuable things are carefully protected. Don't just let anyone have access to you and your personal world. We will talk more about this in Tool 4.

Regardless of why you are online, it's important to have a code of ethics by which you post:

1. What do you promise you will or will not do online? Parents, talk through these things with your kid and then develop a general rule and guidance that applies regardless of where your child is online.

2. Will you post to optimize algorithms?

3. Will you share sensational stories or use copy as clickbait?

4. Will you allow your platform to be used to collect data that isn't provided with the express consent of others or necessary for the management of your growing platform?

5. Will you monetize your content through targeted ads?

6. Will you use your platform to shine light on positive and important stories?

7. Will you use your posts wisely, knowing that even posts that "disappear" quickly (SnapChat, Instagram, or Facebook Stories) have power to impact others?

8. Will you be cognizant of the impact of your post on the lives of others?

In summary, your brand automatically defines who you are, what you care about, and what you take responsibility for. It's indicative of the way you live your life and the types of decisions you make. Now that you've really thought about your child's brand, make sure all pieces align—from their online photos, username, bio, public vs private status, and all-around engagement. Don't wait until your child is getting ready for college or applying for a job to start thinking about the image they've portrayed. Start today and make sure that from their very first post, they are committed to who they are, why they are online.

Exercise 6:
Search Your Brand

I always encourage parents and students to take time to do internet searches on themselves regularly. Know what is out there and what others will find when they look you or your child up. Start with Google of course, but also search sites like bing.com, duckduckgo.com, peekyou.com, zabasearch.com, pipl.com, yoname.com, and spokeo.com. Each of these have indexed information differently, which is why it's important to search more than one search engine. Also, place your/their name in quotes, but after that, expand your search based on operators. This search can look like this:

"FirstName LastName" > What information can I find online about this person

"Firstname Lastname@" > Find possible email addresses associated with this person

"Firstname lastname" filetype:doc > Any word documents that contain this person's name

If you do find personal information, investigate how you can have it deleted. Some sites provide some type of "opt-out" form that allows the user to request its removal. But don't ever count on that being a solution. Remember—once something is online, it's always online.

For older teens or college students who may be launching new profiles on LinkedIn or various job search apps, these platforms inherently require a more professional image, but remember, at the end of the day, everything posted, across all platforms, will be viewed. Brand must be consistent.

TOOL 1 / SUMMARY

- One of the biggest keys to taking hold of this online world starts with you and your child developing their brand, defining it clearly, and anchoring it.

- Your brand is one of the most powerful tools you have right now. Remember, your audience is looking at your online presence and constantly drawing conclusions based on your brand—which is you. People will zoom in on photos to see what liquid is in your red plastic cup, or try and determine if your pupils look dilated. They will note things and pass judgment based on what they believe they saw, whether they were right or not.

- We cannot make everyone happy. We cannot control people who skew things. But we can go from an attitude of posting "whatever and whenever," to posting and sharing with clarity, purpose, and understanding the why and the what—no matter where you find yourself online.

CHAPTER 7:

Tool 2: Define Your Community

Most kids have lots of people in their online community–and they have no idea who they are. That's when they become vulnerable.

Now that you have defined your son or daughter's brand, and the parameters around what they are presenting to the world, we now need to define *who* they are saying it to.

This is Tool 2: Define Your Community. Most kids have lots of people in their online community, and they have no idea who they are or why they are connected and that's when they become vulnerable. So let's pull the curtain back and take a look at who is in your child's online community.

A "FRIEND" ISN'T ALWAYS A FRIEND

Lindsay[70] has an incredible family. Her dad is an executive and her mom is a homemaker. They are involved in their local church and live in a big, beautiful suburban home and the kids attend great schools. While all these things carry weight and create a loosely warranted sense of safety in the "real

---

70 Names changed for purposes of this story

CHAPTER SEVEN

world," it doesn't count for much in the online world. She's an incredible girl; beautiful, friendly, kind, and good-hearted. Like most girls her age, she is active on social media. SnapChat was the platform where she would be noticed and targeted. "He" was older, a known human trafficker to law enforcement, but completely unknown to innocent girls online. Offline, some would call him a pimp, but to her, he was just another connection, follower, and online friend. The truth is, he had noticed her months earlier, targeted her, and took his time to get to her.

Lindsay's dutiful parents were in the habit of actively monitoring their two children, more as a matter of principle than anything else. They weren't aware of any real dangers. They checked their phones, had their passwords, had GPS on their cars, and FaceTimed them often when they were out. But none of that was a match for the online predator to which this teen had unknowingly opened a door.

On the evening of April 30th, she told her parents she was going to the gym. While there, she learned of a party via social media. She decided to have a friend pick her up from the gym and take her to the party. She would leave her car and phone her parent's tracked behind. When curfew approached, she found herself eager to head back to the gym so she could make it home in time, but none of her friends were willing to take her back. Like most teens, she turned to her online world. She borrowed a friend's phone and logged in to her SnapChat account and asked, "Is there anyone in the area who can take me to my car?" He replied, "Sure, on my way." Finally, he would get his prey. He picked her up from the party, but he did not take her back to the gym. As evening turned to morning, Lindsay's parents began their desperate search to find her. The trafficking abuse she endured in the days that followed is simply too difficult to describe. Thanks to the work of her family and law enforcement, Lindsay was found weeks later. She had been drugged, branded, and raped more times than one could imagine, She would never be the same.

Her story, one so painful yet sadly not totally uncommon, forever stands as a reminder that the online world harbors people whose lives and motives are so unfathomably different from our own and who have connected with our children for reasons too grave to understand.

There's a universal truth that says you are the company you keep. We understand this in face-to-face social circles, at school, work or in public. But we often don't make the same connections in the online world. Kids, for that matter, really only see their online community as "assets" in this virtual game of harvesting followers, connections, and "likes." These realities create an opening for problems, which is why Tool 2 is so critical. In the offline world, kids gauge communities all the time, whether at school, camp, or work. They instinctively understand that the company they keep brings forth conversations that they either like or don't like and that the people they associate with affect their image

CHAPTER SEVEN

or reputation (their brand). Kids know to back away from those they don't want to associate with and how to embrace those who align with them socially. It's instinctively clear in a physical setting, however kids completely fail to connect these same truths a in the digital world. Why? Well, for the most part, they tend to operate in the dark. They are stripped of all the in-person cues that activate their instincts. There isn't the benefit of the full engagement of all their senses, and yet they connect in more personal ways, more consistently with their online community than they do with those in their physical community.

Kids are also failing to understand that they are both part of a digital world and leaders of a digital world. That world, although never fully seen, defines them, influences them, brands them, shapes them, and targets them—all in both positive and negative ways. They are part of others' communities when they visit a page or spend time in various online spaces. They are part of others' communities when they choose to follow, like, or comment on the posts of others. But they are leaders of their own online community when they initiate a post or digital activity.

When it comes to community, we must constantly keep in mind that the online world is filled with people with both good and evil intentions. As we navigate this tool of defining your child's online community, we cannot forget your child's brand and purpose. Their community size almost instantly starts to take shape as soon as a child understands these two things. So let's dig into Tool 2. We need to understand who is in our child's online community, what they will inherently be exposed to, and how this reaches our children. We also must keep in mind the sheer magnitude of the platforms our kids are on. With hundreds of millions of users on any given platform, when you child logs on they are connected to every type of person. No one is screening accounts or weeding out who is on a particular platform or monitoring their actions or motives. No one is checking age, doing background checks, banning dangerous people, or keeping them from having multiple accounts. Therefore, we need our kids to understand the many different types of people who might be in their community, and how to respond when red flags arise. This is critical. Let's start with the basics.

THE "WHY" DETERMINES THE "WHO"

The reason your child is online combined with the way they define their brand and present themselves, especially on social media platforms, attracts the people who want to join their community. If your child's goal is to be famous, or create a large following, or look popular, their community will be filled with people they know personally, acquaintances they don't know well, and strangers they do not know at all. And I'm sorry, a "friend of a friend" is still defined as a stranger, no matter how many friends you have in common.

Keep in mind, it's very common for kids to have multiple accounts that parents may or may not know about. They also create accounts for their pets, their alter egos, to "stalk" people, and more. While the brand conversation is still important for those accounts, the community conversation is absolutely critical for all accounts. Maybe your child has decided to be a bit more exclusive, and they will not let as many people into their community. While most kids feel invincible or immortal, your child may challenge this idea and doesn't want "weirdos" following them. This will mean creating a limited community. They are not interested in the pressures of celebrity or online fame, and they will have an easier time navigating the online community. Notice I said, "easier" but not entirely without risk. Regardless of your child's intent, brand, or purpose for being online, all kids must be hyper-vigilant of the dangerous territory that comes with all online communities.

WHAT IS COMMUNITY?

A community consists of people you know, have things in common with, have places in common, have similar rules and standards, or have common attitudes or interests. For example, a church community, sporting community, civic organization, society, sisterhood, or brotherhood. In the offline world, you are tied to a community through reciprocity. There is a mutual benefit for the members of the community. The online community is different. While it is still considered a community, it ties very different people together for no apparent reason than to have an online connection. This online connection opens the door to contact and engagement, even though everything else that would normally tie two people together may be lacking. In short, our kids connect with people online they would never choose to connect with, or engage with, or speak with in person.

CATEGORIES OF CONNECTIONS

People in online communities fall into one of three categories: Known, acquaintances, or unknown.

1. **Known Person:** A known person is someone you known in real life and have spent real time with. Here's the thing, parents—yikes!—a known person can also be someone your child has spent time with online, face-to-face together virtually. They have FaceTimed or had video chats. They could be in the same class or perhaps met through another friend. I know this is uncomfortable, but this is a new reality of the way people are getting to know each other. But I would only put an online connection in this category if they have had virtual face time or in-person conversations.

2. **Acquaintance:** An acquaintance is different. This is someone you are familiar with but do not know on a personal level. It might be the person you see often at the ball field, church, or the grocery store.

3. **Unknown:** In the online world, an unknown person

is someone you have not met in person or only had superficial engagement with. That's the key. It is critical that our kids know that even if they have one hundred friends in common, that person is still a stranger if they've never engaged with them face-to-face directly. Those people are considered "unknown."

Among those known, acquaintances, and unknown, your online community will have people who:

- Follow you
- You follow
- You collaborate with
- Appear on your pages, and your posts appear on theirs
- You play games with
- You video chat with
- You engage with in other ways online (comment, DM, text, share)

It follows that your community is your group, your team. It is a reflection of who you are and the values you hold. The way you interact with your community directly ties to your brand. If you're focused on being a business brand (i.e., a commodity), your goal is to make your community large. However, remember that you'll eventually be praised or "tarred" based on this very same community. It's important to manage who is following you, commenting on your posts, and engaging with you. If your brand is simply about you and your life, then this sense of community is even more critical to home in on and it's best to be more exclusive. For kids who just want to connect with friends and aren't interested in building a large following, your community guidelines are simple: Don't accept people you don't physically know. Even if you think you are only connecting with friends, your online community can be very dangerous. Before accepting a friend request, each child should ask "How do I know this person? Have I been to their house? Do I know their parents? How long have I known them? Would my parents approve?"

THINK ABOUT IT

The magnitude of the world wide web is beyond comprehension. I've said it before and it bears repeating—once your child is online, they are connected to the entire world, and the entire world is connected to them. This is both wonderful and frightening. When pulling a community together from a pool of the whole wide world, the choices are vast.

These three types of people—known, acquaintances, and unknown—come from the following:
- Family
- Friends
- Offline acquaintances—kids and adults you have seen in real life and are familiar with but don't know well.

CHAPTER SEVEN

- Online acquaintances which are strangers—people you have never seen or met but think you know, as you share contacts.
- Teachers
- Coaches
- Future, current, or past school/college people. Staff, friends, professors, admissions
- People from within your parents' network
- People from your career path
- Future job or business opportunities
- Strangers who are wonderful
- Strangers who keep to themselves but watch you
- Strangers who are very bad (traffickers and groomers)
- Predators who seek images
- Predators who seek to exploit images
- Predators who seek to make actual contact
- Criminals falling under every possible category
- Drug dealers
- Stalkers and trolls
- Those suffering from addiction to games, pornography, drugs, alcohol.

- Those who are abusive to partners, family, friends, and strangers.
- Those hurting badly who want to target and hurt others.
- Those who are suicidal.
- Hackers
- Scammers
- Bots
- Fake Accounts
- Those seeking to take your identity.
- And more

What tools do you use in real life to keep your kids safe from people you don't want them to associate with? Can you create similar tools for the online world? The goal here is to raise your child's awareness of who to communicate with, who to block, or how to keep certain followers safely at bay. What will your parameters be for deciding who will get into your child's inner circle? Will your child willingly talk to people who message them? Did the family create rules around in-app messaging earlier on in the book? I hope so! But the main question goes back to this: How can you ultimately keep yourself safe from the community made up of people that are truly unknown to you? Your community isn't a third party, separate from you. Your community includes you, your community engages with you, and that engagement has consequences, which we'll discuss in our next tool. But by bringing someone, anyone, into your community, they have a level of potential power they didn't have when they were outside of your community.

In general, once you add a person to your community, they can:

- Talk to you

- Call you

- Find you via your exact location (Remember, most apps have GPS tracking. Did the family come up with rules when it comes to turning GPS tracking on or off?)

- Physically hurt you

- Mentally hurt you

- Offer you things you shouldn't be offered (drugs, pills, elicit material)

- Take what you're posting and do anything they want with it—share it, comment on it, make it their own.

Additionally, most social media platforms don't offer any protection of your brand or image. Many allow for what's called "parody accounts" or accounts that mimic you, use some of your photos, or talk about you. Yes, fake accounts can be reported and removed by the platform, but parody accounts are allowed by some social media platforms. I can't express this enough—what's posted on the internet stays on the internet, even if unintended. Your community can do whatever they want with what you share online. It's public, period.

Exercise 7:
Three Red Flags in Communities

As you can see, if your child has an online community, protecting them is difficult, regardless of who is in their community. So let's start by creating rules that they can understand and follow. Let's start with the three major red flags that everyone online needs to understand. Remember, if you find it difficult to go over the following material with your child, then they are not mature enough to handle the realities of the online world, and they shouldn't be online on any platform.

- **Community Red Flag #1:** An unknown person or acquaintance wants to meet them in person or asks for personal information, where they are, or where they live. We must teach our kids to be mindful of direct vs indirect questions. A direct question looks like this: "Hey! Where do you live?" An indirect question looks like this: "Hey, I think you live near the mall, but send me your address. I want to mail you something I think you'll love!" Additionally, your child should never share their school or its location. A direct question could be: "What school did you say you go to?" Or an indirect question could be: "What's your school's football team called?" Never share your place of business and be mindful of questions like "What hours did you say you were working at the mall?" or "Ugh, I can't believe you have to work this weekend, at the mall, right?" It follows that if a child has posted or shared this information which allows an unknown person to bypass the process of asking, your child must immediately share with you or a trusted adult if an unknown online connection shows up at any private or personal location.

- **Community Red Flag #2:** Your child is getting requests from anyone for inappropriate pictures, videos, text messages, or content of any manner. This happens way more often than anyone would like to acknowledge, but we must acknowledge it. Your kids need to feel safe enough to come to you even if they made a poor choice and sent something anyway. Remember, kids will do things out of character in the pressure of the moment.

- **Community Red Flag #3:** Someone from their community starts talking about or sharing inappropriate content with them, including sexual content, drug-related content, illegal activity, or dangerous challenges. Make discussing these issues as safe and welcome as possible.

Beyond sharing the major red flags with your child, your child must also agree to contact you or a designated trusted adult whenever they come across this activity from people within their community.

DEFINE YOUR COMMUNITY

THE REALITIES AROUND PREDATORS

Parents, did you know: According to the FBI, there are an estimated 500,000 online predators actively targeting and grooming each day? Over 50% of online sexual exploitation is of teens 12–15 years old, as they are easily groomed and more likely to connect online with people unknown to them. Where do predators go? Everywhere but a majority focus on chatrooms and private messaging. Children will usually be asked for a sexually explicit photo or, in extreme cases, will be asked to meet in person or get on the phone. Despite the dangers, while using social media, 40% of children said they would remove privacy settings to attract more friends or followers. Children younger than 12 are aware these things take place but need more talking to. Only 20% of 8–11 year-olds are aware of these safety issues and are concerned that strangers may find out information about them. That said, nearly 60% of parents are concerned about online strangers.[71] Parents, you may be thinking, "I see the numbers, but does this really happen? In real life?" The answer is yes, and it's important that you know this and that you talk to your kids about it using real stories. Sadly, I have countless such stories, but here are three:

- **Washington State:** A 34-year-old man admitted he planned to rape a young girl, age 13, who he met online. Richland Police arrested the suspect.

---

[71] https://childsafety.losangelescriminallawyer.pro/children-and-grooming-online-predators.html

CHAPTER SEVEN

- **California:** A 36-year-old woman faked her age, identity, and photo, in order to create an online relationship with a 13-year-old boy she chatted with in an Xbox live chat room. The woman asked to meet the boy, allegedly flying from California to Maryland to rape him.

- **California:** A 24-year-old man is accused of kidnapping, raping, and killing a 13-year-old girl he met on social media. The two began texting and exchanging photos. They eventually met in person. The suspect allegedly kidnapped the young victim, sexually assaulted her, and then set her body on fire.

We also know that predators will infiltrate a child's online network, sending friend requests to their friends, in an effort to look more familiar to the child and get them to accept the predator's friend request directly. Predators will also capitalize on a major achievement in your child's life to gain access to them, with the intent of getting inappropriate content from your child.

Take this story: A local little league baseball team made it to the Little League World Series. The local news covered their journey. Parents gave the media permission for the children's faces to be shown as they practiced and that was all the child predators needed in order to pounce. The news stories gave the location of the team so the predators began following them. Soon, they started befriending or following the players on social media pretending to be college baseball scouts. In their excitement, the kids let their guards down and started engaging with them. It was only when one the of "college scouts" asked for a photo of the child where the scout could see his "muscles" that the child got suspicious and told his parents. The parents discovered what was happening and blocked the predators and reported them to local law enforcement.

Exercise 8:
Community Review

So let's keep talking about this. We've learned about online communities in general, but what does your child's online community look like? Let's do a deep dive.

1. First of all, which platforms are your child really on? Do you know? And are they sharing their true list with you? Are they including any fake accounts or accounts they have made for other things like their pets, artwork, creative projects, etc.?

2. How many people are following them on their various accounts?

3. Of those following them, how many would they say they know (have seen and engaged with in real life or at length virtually)? How many are unknown to them? Can you turn this into a percentage just so you are aware? Out of 1,000 followers, how many does your child know

CHAPTER SEVEN

in real life or even virtually?

4. Of those unknown, what are the demographics? Men vs women, age, location? The apps can break this down for you, especially if you have public accounts. This information will be helpful as you create rules around your child's online community.

Now that you've done a basic inventory, what should your strategy be moving forward? Your community defines you, but how you build and handle your community depends on your brand. If your child is online to be famous, or get noticed, or be seen, and they are trying to develop a large community, the question becomes: How do they do this while protecting themselves physically and mentally? (Hint: You will need to step up your protection game plan; we will get to that in a little bit.) Remember, they will ultimately be defined by members of their community, and their posts will eventually be viewed under a microscope. Everything they post, like, follow, and anything they share—every online engagement is there for consumption, opinion, praise, and ridicule, going all the way back to the first post. Look at Charli D'Amelio. The teen now has 121.9 million followers on TikTok and to date has shared 1,833 videos. (That's a lot of work!) In a Yahoo lifestyle feature, D'Amelio shared that criticism of her "every move" is difficult: "It's hard."[72] In fact, both Charli and her

---

72 https://www.yahoo.com/lifestyle/charli-damelio-famous-friendships-223328275.html

sister Dixie discuss the toll this has taken on them in their documentary The D'Amelio Show (Hulu). Additionally, with fame comes headlines like this: "Many of TikTok's biggest stars aren't viewed favorably by the public, according to a poll conducted by Insider and SurveyMonkey."[73]

Know this, be equipped for it, and have a strategy. Make sure your child knows if they cast a wider net, or have allowed unlimited people into their community, they must be smarter and sharper with their posts—safety minded first and foremost—which we will dive into more in Tool 4.

If they are online only to connect with friends and socialize, they still must also be protective of their community. The same rules apply, but the majority of their followers should be personally known. That said, some kids will fall somewhere in between. They don't want to be famous, but they do want to be seen, consumed, trend, and have a large following. They also need to closely follow the guidance we will get to in Tool 4.

Parents, I know this is a hard topic, especially since the online world is rewiring our kids to open the doors to their world and accept everyone in.

Beyond having honest conversations on why your child is online and what they hope to achieve online, there's a rule that applies to everyone and it's simple: Don't hang out with the wrong crowd online.

---

[73] https://www.insider.com/tiktok-stars-liked-influencer-loren-gray-bella-poarch-charli-damelio-2021-9

CHAPTER SEVEN

If your child has public accounts and accepts every friend and follower request, you must have firm rules on who they engage with and teach them why, when, and how to block people. Those with private accounts who are not "harvesting followers" should be encouraged to examine their friends and followers list regularly, and take the time to delete superficial connections or those they do not fully know and trust, and those they simply aren't going to ever talk to again. Notice friends who become foes! Remember the three red flags and really live by them. And no matter what, always be mindful of how personal your posts are.

TOOL 2 / SUMMARY

- Kids often fail to see they are part of a massive online community.
- Anyone you connect with or engage with makes up your online community.
- Once connected, you are associated with each other.
- The reason you are online determines how vast your online community is, which creates safety concerns.
- The people in your online community, those known and those completely unknown, will all have access to you.
- Your online community is filled with people who have a variety of intentions: some good, some really evil.
- Your online community will expose you to a whole host of things: wonderful things to very dangerous things, to life threatening things.

CHAPTER 8:

Tool 3: Develop an Exit Strategy

Kids need an exit strategy from the threats they will encounter. The key is to "Know it, recognize it, and block it."

As we know, there are all kinds of dangers in the online world and in this chapter, we are going to look more at the specific types of dangers, and the universal reality of what our kids can expect to face on a daily basis. Tool 3 is about having conversations with our kids to give them an "out" or an exit strategy–from potentially harmful situations. The key is to "know it, recognize it, and block it." To be forewarned is to be forearmed. The old adage "Sticks and stones can break my bones, but words can never hurt me" could now be literally changed to "Sticks and stones can break my bones, but words can end my life." On top of the blatantly dangerous predators, words and the ease in which they are exchanged online can have a larger-than-life impact on most youth, and many parents have no idea about the magnitude of their child's struggle in this area. On social media, people say things that they would never say in real life. Looking at the consequences of the online world and identifying when your child will need an exit strategy is critical, and it may literally save their life.

CHAPTER EIGHT

Because there are so many potential harms, I've broken this information down into two categories—external threats and internal threats. First, we'll cover the external threats, or things that bombard our kids from the outside world. Then, we'll look at the impact of the internal threats, which are the thoughts, habits, addictions, potentially harmful choices, and other issues kids will develop internally based on their engagement in the online landscape.

> **PARENTAL ADVISORY:** Now, parents, if you've been reading this book along with your child, let me add a disclaimer here. This will be our toughest and most explicit chapter, so you may want to read ahead alone and then determine how to engage your child. All of it must be discussed with all children who are online, but the best way to do that will be based on their age and maturity, as we indicated earlier.

Let me begin with a personal story...

I have an online presence. I am on Twitter, Facebook, TikTok, SnapChat, and Instagram. I only use three of these regularly, but I have accounts on all five. I represent a brand, Crime Stoppers of Houston. I'm the face of it, so all of my accounts are public. I create digital content personally and through third-party interviews, and I share those videos online. I am purposefully trying to cast as large a net as possible to share our messaging about safety with as many people as possible. Due to Covid and the virtual world we all live in,

I also have a Skype account that I use only for TV interviews. To that end, I have only shared my Skype ID with TV producers.

That said, a few months ago, I was in a Zoom meeting with one of my colleagues when I got a Skype call that took me by surprise. Again, I only use this account for TV interviews which are all scheduled. When the call notification popped up, I noticed that I had also missed a call from that same Skype handle minutes before. *Did I fail to put an interview on my calendar? Who else would be calling me on this dedicated account?* Thoughts like this and others (*Shoot!*) were running through my head. I excused myself from my Zoom meeting and accepted the Skype call. The screen was dark at first and there was an awkward moment of "hellos." I could hear something, but I could not make out who was there. Eventually, the caller's camera went from black to full video and the content before me was shocking. This was not a TV producer calling me. This was someone completely unknown to me, and what I saw had me aghast! Before me lay a naked man with the camera centered on his private parts as he pleased himself. I was taken aback, and frantically began "ending" the call.

The entire experience was thirty-two seconds from start to finish, but I was left sitting there feeling disgusted, offended, and truthfully, violated. And then a Skype message came through asking me—a mother of three daughters—for an "inappropriate" photo. I got angry. *Very angry.*

CHAPTER EIGHT

I'm an adult, and while offended and disgusted, I could process what took place and move on. But what about your child?

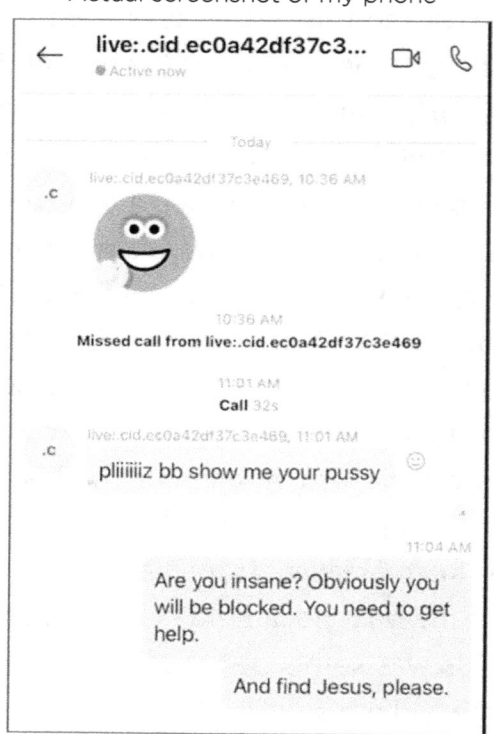

Actual screenshot of my phone

> live:.cid.ec0a42df37c3...
> Active now
>
> Today
>
> live:.cid.ec0a42df37c3e469, 10:36 AM
>
> 10:36 AM
> **Missed call from live:.cid.ec0a42df37c3e469**
>
> 11:01 AM
> **Call** 32s
>
> live:.cid.ec0a42df37c3e469, 11:01 AM
> pliiiiiz bb show me your pussy
>
> 11:04 AM
> Are you insane? Obviously you will be blocked. You need to get help.
>
> And find Jesus, please.

How would they have handled that? In the moments following this encounter, all I could think about was the many young tweens and teens around the globe who may have also innocently answered a video call, something so universally normal for them, only to be faced with such inappropriate and in-your-face explicit content. That got me even angrier.

At any moment, in this world of "click, click, click," any

one of those clicks can be immediately damaging and dangerous to a vulnerable young mind. I wondered, How many young kids may have stopped to watch? Even just out of curiosity? How many wouldn't know what to do? How many would freeze in panic? How many may have been intrigued and even followed up with photos when asked? How many? What would your child have done? Do you know? Do they? The online world is filled with people who are not well and have dark intentions. All of our kids will be exposed to these people and their content on a regular basis, especially the kids who are online with the goal of gaining followers/subscribers and who seek to cast a wide net to gain a following. My goal is to navigate you and your children through these tricky waters, coming out on the other side with tools and strategies to combat these dangerous external bombardments from the online world. So, in addition to identifying the biggest issues our kids can encounter, we want to talk about the impact and a strategy to protect them before and after the bombardment. Let's dive in.

ARM THEM WITH KNOWLEDGE

I've been saying it from the start: We must be talking to our kids about what they will be exposed to, even though it's difficult to talk about, and empower them with an exit strategy from harmful engagements. We do not want our kids to panic or dig around with curiosity, or consume harmful content, or accept invitations to do things without understanding what's right or wrong, or flat out dangerous. We want them to think through real situations, understand the issues, and define them in advance so that when they are confronted, they will know what to do and not fall victim to the pressure of the moment. To skip this step and ignore the issues is to leave them treading in dangerous waters alone. The propensity to find themselves in harmful situations is the very reason experts want kids to stay off social media and out of the digital world altogether. I wish that could be the case, but it will never be realistic for an entire generation of kids already being raised in the digital age. So, in this tool we'll be challenging our kids to examine their role in any online encounter–participant, enabler, bystander, or disrupter–and create an appropriate response plan: Exit or delete; report to school, parents, police, and platforms; or block. Let's dig in...

WHAT IS YOUR ROLE IN THE ENCOUNTER?

There are four basic roles in any encounter:

1. **Participant:** This refers to someone who is actively engaging in online activity. You participate by liking (affirming), posting, sharing, expanding the content to your own community, or adding affirming commentary. This is a serious position to take if the encounter or action is questionable. A participant can get in grave trouble with their school (remember, most schools

DEVELOP AN EXIT STRATEGY

have a "student code of conduct" that can be broken by a student's online participation). They can get into legal trouble for posting threatening content or hateful speech. In many places, anyone age 10 and over can be charged for criminal behavior, which encompasses online statements, threats, or actions. Beyond that, a participant carries the impact of their engagement for a lifetime, especially in the current climate we live in. If you are choosing to be a participant in questionable posts or activity, know that your actions carry tremendous consequences.

2. **Enabler:** This person sees what is happening and actively allows it to continue. They do not block, they do not report it, or encourage the activity to stop. Instead, they feed into it by liking another person's post. An enabler may face certain ramifications for a "like" depending on the content.

3. **Bystander:** This person sees what is going on but stays quiet or neutral. They neither participate, nor enable, nor stop the activity from taking place. In their silence, they allow the negative activity to continue. They fail to block, report, or encourage the activity to stop. Bystanders may never face school punishment, criminal or civil liability, or the loss of an opportunity due to an online negative action. Still they may face guilt or shame for not doing the right thing.

4. **Disrupter:** This person takes action to break the cycle

of bad behavior. They do not share, like, or positively engage. Instead, they block, report, and thwart negative or dangerous behavior.

LET'S TALK ABOUT IT

Ask your child about these four roles and what it means to them. Ask them to define them in their own words and give examples. Make it part of the family plan that they consciously think about what type of person they will be when they engage in the online world and what the consequences and duties are for each role.

We know that the younger kids are when they start using social media, online gaming, streaming, and other digital services, the greater the impact these platforms have on them and their mental health. We know that the amount of time they spend on gadgets affects them in several ways. We know that many tweens/teens are navigating this dangerous online world while simultaneously going through intense physical and emotional changes.

And here's more: We also know that gender plays a role in how kids manage the aggression that may come from being online. For example, studies have shown that teen males who feel aggression are more apt to lash out physically, either through sports, aggressive digital gaming, or an actual fight with a friend or sibling. Teen girls who feel aggression are more apt to lash out socially, either through social retaliation, excluding or targeting others in school or online, or creating or sharing rumors or secrets with the goal of hurting others. This is why we must give them an out when the pressure becomes too much. In the next exercise, we are going to bring awareness to the impact the online world may already be having as you talk through the following questions with your child.

Exercise 9:
Examining External Threats

1. How old were you when you started going online, using social media, or gaming?

2. Was that the right age for you to start? In looking back, would you have liked to start earlier or later?

3. Where do you spend most of your time online?

    a. Social media

    b. Gaming

    c. Creating content

    d. Something else

4. How much time do you spend on social media (in hours per day)? By the way, parents, are you okay with their answer here?

CHAPTER EIGHT

    a. How does it make you feel?

    b. Happy

    c. Sad

    d. Angry, frustrated

    e. Lonely

    f. Connected

    g. Seen

    h. Scared

    i. Weak, powerful, important, insecure

    j. Something else

5. How much time do you spend gaming (in hours per day)? By the way, parents, are you okay with their answer here?

6. How does it make you feel?

    a. Happy

    b. Social

    c. Excited

    d. Content

    e. Like you are doing something

    f. Angry

    g. Aggressive

    h. Frustrated

    i. Addicted

    j. Restless

    k. Scared

    l. Something else

7. Are you aware that your time online and gaming affects how you feel?

    a. Yes

    b. No

    c. Don't think about it

    d. Don't think it does

There are no right or wrong answers here. This is just an exercise to get us talking about these issues and thinking about the impact. As you work through these conversations, write down what your child answers and how they are feeling. I would also suggest verifying their screen time by checking their devices. Are the on more than they realize? I'd also check back a few times a year to see if their feelings toward the online world, digital consumption, or gaming has changed and how they presently feel.

CHAPTER EIGHT

KEY EXTERNAL THREATS

Now let's take a look at the key external threats. I say "key" because there's no way to make an exhaustive list. That's why we have to raise our kids' awareness, empowering them to make healthy decisions anytime they recognize that something is a threat or when find themselves in a heightened emotional state or feeling vulnerable.

ONLINE STALKING (CYBERSTALKING)/HARASSMENT

When we were children, we worried about bullies on the playground, but there was safety in numbers. Today, the opposite is true. Today's youth deal with that plus cyberbullies, cyberstalking, and harassment. Kids share a lot of personal content online and unknowingly open the door for others to "consume" them—follow their lives, their world, and form strong attachments, either for or against them. Others can feel like a part of their world or become obsessed with outcomes. In addition to those unknown to our children but who follow our kids online, we also must navigate regular friendships, acquaintances, frenemies, enemies, and more.

Consider the stalking and killing of Bianca Devins. Bianca and her family lived in a small town in upstate New York. She became well known for her Instagram page under the name @escty. She was a 17-year-old Instagram celebrity and so-called "egirl." She had just graduated from high school and was excited to attend a local college in the fall.

DEVELOP AN EXIT STRATEGY

She developed an offline relationship with someone she met online and one night, the two were together at a concert. The night ended tragically when Bianca was graphically and brutally murdered. Her "friend" had most likely been cyberstalking her for a long time. What made the case even more horrifying was that the teen killer posted images of the slaying on Instagram, the gaming website Discord, and 4chan—including an extremely graphic and bloody image of the victim sitting in an SUV with her neck cut. The caption read, "Sorry [expletive], you're gonna have to find someone else to orbit." (The term orbit is used to describe men who lurk on a woman's social media account in hopes of having sex with her).

Cyberstalking occurs when someone uses any electronic means (text, email, website, social media, phone) to harass, control, manipulate, or habitually disparage another with or without a direct or implied threat of physical harm. The cyberstalker seeks to exert power and control by using verbal, emotional, sexual, or social abuse. If ignored, this can become extremely dangerous for all. So, what's our child's exit strategy? Our children need to be able to identify this type of threat. Would they know it if they were a victim of it? If they are the target, the key is that they recognize it and report it. What if they saw this happening to someone else online? What role would they play then? Would they be a participant, enabler, bystander, or disrupter? I hope they would choose disrupter—every time.

CHAPTER EIGHT

What are some ways they can stop this type of activity?

- Never like or share the harasser's post.
- Always take screenshots.
- Always, report the activity.

If you are the target:

- Stop all communication with the harasser; it's important to not respond.
- Block the harasser from your phone, email, and social media accounts.
- Seek support from a trusted friend, family member, or a professional counselor.
- Keep a record of the dates, times, people involved, and descriptions of when the stalking occurred. You may need to provide this information when you file a report.
- Save and print screenshots, emails, and text messages as evidence.
- Report the incidents, with the details, to the website company or cell phone service provider.
- Call 911 if you are ever in immediate harm.

DEVELOP AN EXIT STRATEGY

- If you are concerned about your own safety or the safety of someone else involved in a dangerous relationship, visit the National Domestic Violence Hotline to chat or call 800-799-7233.[74]

SEXTORTION & BLACKMAIL

Sextortion is a form of sexual exploitation and sadly, it happens more often than parents realize. So, how does a child get tied up in this? A child either believes the predator has inappropriate content that the predator got, unbeknownst to the child, or the child, engaging with someone online that they "thought" they knew, willingly sends inappropriate content, only to then have the content used against them. It goes something like this:

The Random Email: A child receives an email in which the sender claims to have been "watching" them through the child's phone camera or computer camera. The sender then demands cash or Bitcoin in exchange for keeping the private content private. The kid panics and tries to engage or handle the situation alone. This is a huge no-no. What we want kids to understand is that when received randomly, nine times out of ten (or even ten times out of ten), no one has hacked their system or taken any videos, photos, or data. These are scam emails looking for payments of cash or Bitcoin.

---

[74] Fightcybercrime.org

CHAPTER EIGHT

Ignore the emails, block the sender's email account, and delete the emails.

Real Engagement Has Taken Place: Other examples are more concerning. We know that kids often do end up engaging with others online and sometimes sharing inappropriate content. This creates a difference in power between the child and the person who requested the inappropriate content. After a child has innocently sent a video or picture, the perpetrator often will demand more content or threaten to share whatever has already been received with the child's family and network. Sadly, this happens more than you think. Children in these cases feel overwhelmed, alone, and severely traumatized. In extreme cases, children feel trapped and are forced to do more, including create sexual content or perform sexual acts via real time streaming. Many of these children find themselves in a web they cannot escape and grow more entangled with every photo or video.

Take the story of Riley K. Basford, a 15-year-old, living in his father's Texas home. The family came to learn that Basford had been extorted online after he shared personal photographs with a Facebook user posing as a young, attractive girl. The perpetrator demanded $3,500 from Basford after photos were exchanged; threatening to share the photos with Basford's friends and family. The young boy couldn't handle the situation and chose suicide as a way out.[75]

---

75   https://www.nny360.com/communitynews/healthmatters/he-did-not-want-to-die-family-of-potsdam-15-year-old-who-died-by/article_38cb3143-603f-5927-8aaf-d2491f194915.html

DEVELOP AN EXIT STRATEGY

It's so hard to talk about these things, but we must. Kids must be made aware that these are mass emails and the senders are waiting for anyone to respond. They are scamming whomever they can for money. Kids should never fall for these types of emails! In the second scenario, the predator targeted a child and did whatever was necessary to make the child believe they had a special connection. In these scenarios, a kid may actually know the requester in real life (it may be a boyfriend/girlfriend situation) or they may only "think" they know the requester because they've spent a lot of time chatting with them. In all cases, regardless of who is asking or why, a request for inappropriate photos or videos is a huge red flag and must always be answered with a "No." We are creating a preemptive exit strategy in these situations by talking through the different scenarios in advance. Children should never participate, enable, or be a bystander in these situations. They must always be a disrupter.

If a child makes a mistake and sends an inappropriate photo or video, the key is to make sure they are comfortable to come to you (or another trusted adult) for help to get out of the situation. As the adult, always remain calm. Remember, tweens and teens will do things that are out of character. They need to feel safe to come to you when they realize they've done the wrong thing. Also, never pay ransom or send more content. Always report the offender to the authorities (and you can do this quietly). Always report the offender to the social media carriers, and immediately take the child to counseling to deal with the very real trauma this causes. Kids who have been taken advantage of in this way often feel ashamed, embarrassed, afraid, depressed, betrayed, guilty, alone, angry, overwhelmed, anxious, and scared. Parents, we must be a safe haven for our vulnerable children. Remember, at this age, they make decisions without considering the consequences until it is often too late. But by talking in advance, by sharing the risks and dangers in advance, and giving them every tool necessary to know the danger and see it coming, they can better protect themselves from it. No matter what, as mistakes are made, our position should always be to help our children heal and make better decisions, even if we are shocked by their choices.

Sextortion and sexual harassment are real and rampant. In fact, as late teens and early adults participate in research, we have come to learn that nearly 21% of women ages 18 to 29 report being sexually harassed online; and about 53% of young women ages 18 to 29 say that someone has sent them explicit images they did not ask for.[76] We must protect them and address all the resulting feelings. No shame, no blame— only help for our children who are victims of these times. For more information on sextortion, go to fbi.gov and rain.org.

PREDATORS AND CHILD EXPLOITATION

Cyber-predators don't just see a child online, find their address, and go take them. Once they have a target, they

---

76 https://www.ofsms.org/resources/

will take their time to cultivate a connection with them. The grooming process looks different based on the predator's ultimate objective. Still, the process follows similar patterns, which includes visiting social media sites, gaming platforms, digital streaming shows, and other online areas popular with young people. The predator will make contact, pretending to be the age of the tween/teen. The predator typically uses fake profile pictures. They study their target and pretend to share similar interests. The predator will spend time liking their posts, occasionally commenting, and making private, but friendly, outreach through messages such as "I saw that you were the lead in your school play, that's cool!" or "It looks like you are upset with a friend, why are people so mean?" Parents, this is a reminder to go over what type of posts your child is making! If they choose to share everything online, they must know that predators will use this content against them. They will spend time and do whatever they can to get personal information (school, home, place of work—remember our 3 Community Red Flags!). They will send gifts or make direct contact with their target or lure their target to them. Throughout the process, the groomer will also start to befriend people in the child's circle. They will use this as future leverage against the child.

Once the predator sees an opportunity, he or she will start steering the chats toward anything sexual. The target will soon repeatedly be asked to take photos or videos of themselves and send them to the groomer. In extreme cases, the groomer will pressure the child to meet in person and even

CHAPTER EIGHT

fly to the child's city to meet in person. As we saw above, once the groomer has photos, the blackmailing process can begin with threats of sharing private sexual chats, photos, or videos with the target's friends or family. Sadly, the process works more often than one thinks, especially with children 12 to 15 who are more susceptible to grooming and manipulation.

I shared some of these stats in the last chapter, but the magnitude of what's happening really needs to be examined:

- There are approximately **500,000** online predators active every day, targeting multiple children at one time.[77]

- A whopping **82% of child sex crimes originate from online social media sites** where predators gain knowledge of their victims' likes and habits.[78]

- Roughly **89%** of sexual advances directed at children occur in **internet chatrooms or through instant messaging.**[79]

Parents, we know this is an issue, with nearly 60% of us reporting being concerned about threats that strangers pose online.[80] It's time we take this difficult issue head on with direct conversations with our little online users. If they want to be online, they must be aware this is happening and know the signs of grooming and what to do about it.

---

77 https://www.wane.com/news/local-news/with-500000-online-predators-active-everyday-heres-how-to-keep-your-kids-safe/
78 https://www.ofsms.org/resources/
79 https://www.guardchild.com/statistics/
80 https://childsafety.losangelescriminallawyer.pro/children-and-grooming-online-predators.html

SIGNS THAT A CHILD IS BEING GROOMED ONLINE

Online grooming may be difficult to detect because it often occurs while a child is home and simply using the computer. Groomers often order children not to talk about their conduct. However, as we really pay attention, we may find signs that a child is being groomed by an online predator. This may include spending increased amounts of time online, becoming secretive about their online conduct, switching screens, or closing tabs or windows whenever a parent is close, changing passwords often, using sexual language they would not be expected to know, and becoming emotionally volatile.

It's very difficult for a child to sniff out a groomer in a sea of exchanges with their online community, especially when a groomer's profile photos, posts, and stories seem so innocent and authentically "teen-centered." Still, groomers are experts at making themselves appear like friends but eventually will try to get very personal (red flag), turn the conversation sexual (red flag), ask personal questions slowly over time or when gaming (red flags), and ask for inappropriate content (sexual chats, photos, or videos) as a joke, dare, or a sign of a "special relationship" (red flag). Rules and conversations around this topic must continually be taking place.

Parents, we need to consistently check in on what our kids are doing online, review our children's followers, and what type of chats come their way. We must talk about the atmosphere of our children's online space, and do it often. Remind kids, even those trying to be famous or build a large brand, to never cultivate relationships with strangers online. Conversations become worrisome when the person on the other side of the screen insists that the relationship be kept hidden from a parent or caretaker (remember your rule on hidden apps!). When a child thinks they know a person they are chatting with online, yet they have never met in real life, the red flags become even more important.

ONLINE TRENDS MAKE ONLINE SOLICITATION OF MINORS ENTICING

Along the same lines, online solicitation of minors increased during Covid (2020). Parents, I cringe writing about this, but we have to address it. Do yourself a favor, take a moment to go on TikTok or Instagram and search the term "sugar daddy" or "sugar baby" (#sugardaddy #sugarbaby). I literally die every time. Yes, this is about the exchange of "time" for gifts and money and sadly, the practice is legal. Obviously sexual favors are asked, which is illegal when dealing with a minor, but perfectly legal for an adult.

Again, no one is monitoring this or checking the ages of the participants. The trend right now is huge online, and our kids all know about it. It feeds into the sinister reality of the online solicitation of minors. Generally speaking, the online solicitation of minors is illegal and includes any action taken by an adult to elicit a sexual response (photos, videos, graphic messages) from a child. This area is more direct and fueled by the global community our children engage with, the great wall of anonymity as well as the many different tools predators have to lure our children. While criminal in nature, these crimes are hard to trace and follow, partially because social media companies protect the identity and content of the user. It's important that kids know these types of things happen and can therefore protect themselves from ever being a target. Additionally, if they see this type of activity affecting someone they know, what role should your child to play? It's certainly scary to get involved in these situations but reporting accounts and being a disrupter is always an easy and safe first step.

LEGAL CONSEQUENCES FOR ONLINE PREDATORS

Threats of violence, child pornography, unauthorized sexually explicit messages or photos, or photos/videos taken in private places should always be reported immediately to your local law enforcement authority. Many states have laws preventing adults from "corrupting" minors or engaging in sexually explicit conversations with those under the age of 18. In addition, it is illegal to send pornographic material to minors or to encourage or pressure minors to send explicit photographs or videos of themselves. Adults who are convicted of this type of conduct can be sentenced to prison and may be required to register as a sex offender as a result of the conviction.

CHAPTER EIGHT

RESOURCES:

For more on federal laws: https://www.justice.gov/criminal-ceos/citizens-guide-us-federal-law-obscenity

For more on sexual offender laws and prevention of sexual violence: https://www.ncbi.nlm.nih.gov/pmc/articles/PMC2820068/

GROOMING EFFECTS ON A CHILD

A child who has been groomed and exploited online will face terrible emotional and physical ramifications. Often, the sheer embarrassment of the ordeal will be too much for them to handle. The fear that their actions will be shared with others in their community will plague them. The feeling of being violated and exploited can lead to eating disorders, social anxiety, self-harm, depression, drug abuse, increased sexual activity, and suicide.

But parents, no child is alone in this. Sadly, 2020 was a record-breaking year, with more than 21.7 million reports of suspected child sexual exploitation made to the National Center on Missing and Exploited Children's CyberTipline.[81] Our children are being hunted online, and we must do all we can to protect them.

---

[81] https://www.missingkids.org/blog/2021/rise-in-online-enticement-and-other-trends--ncmec-releases-2020-

DID THE CHILD RUN AWAY...OR WERE THEY LURED AWAY?

This is a huge area of work for many in the child safety space. I think you'll agree with me when I say that a "runaway" child is handled very differently by law enforcement and seen differently in the community than a child who, let's say, has been "abducted." We look at runaways and say: "They made a choice. They'll come back when they are ready. Little Becky was going through some things. She's a wild child; she'll calm down and come home soon." That type of thinking reduces the massive push to find a runaway child. Guess what? Human traffickers know this and often work this to their advantage.

John Clark, an oil and gas executive and founder of Operation Texas Shield, is also a renowned expert in the fight against human trafficking. He studied and uncovered the process groomers and predators use to recruit and lure away kids and teens. In a Facebook post, he wrote:

> *Sex trafficking often starts with a man or woman a few years older than the targeted teenage girl. The groomer takes the teenager to new places, is fun and acts like a mentor. The groomer then introduces the teenage girl to drugs and alcohol while trying to isolate her from her parents. The teenage girl is then introduced to new people and brought to adult places like clubs. Eventually, the teenager meets a pimp, usually disguised as a musician, club owner or something else exciting to the teenager. After building some rapport, the pimp usually invites the*

teenager to a party after she turns 18. That's the point a teenager is most likely forced into sex trafficking.

He further outlined an actual six-step process that many parents of victims have found to be exactly what happened to their own kids. The alarming truth is that what happens in step six appears like a teen has run away, when in reality, that young adult has been strategically lured away under fraud and false pretense. This clever manipulation detours law enforcement to some degree. While the world somewhat tosses the "runaway" to the side, what's actually happening is that he/she is stuck enduring horrific abuse. Trafficking victims are raped, sold many times a day, injected with drugs against their will, and often tattooed and branded by the trafficker who took them. Knowing these six steps and how to recognize them may very well save your child's life. Here are the six steps as defined by John Clark at fightforus.org[82].

Exercise 10:
The Six-Step Process of Human Traffickers

Parents, I know this is a really difficult reality to face and discuss with your kids, but I am asking you to go through these six steps with them. Let them see what these traffickers do so they can identify it if they see it happening in their life, or the life of a friend.

---
82 https://www.fightforus.org/what-you-need-to-know

DEVELOP AN EXIT STRATEGY

1. **BEFRIEND**: This step is the hardest step to recognize. A new, seemingly non-threatening "friend" strikes up a friendship with your teen. The new friend is typically fun, seems very nice, and often acts as a mentor. Groomers can be anywhere, even at school or church, and some groomers have fake parents or a fake family in a home that is set up only as a facade for the recruiting process.

2. **INTOXICATE**: This step introduces friction in the teen's relationships at home. The new friend's objective is to make sure your child has fun and feels "cool," often by introducing alcohol and/or drugs. The friend (a.k.a. groomer) will increase the frequency and ease of access to alcohol and/or drugs. Your child begins to feel a sense of independence and a desire to fit in because "everyone" is doing the same.

3. **ALIENATE**: This step begins to turn a teen against his or her parents. In front of parents, a groomer will be polite and nice. Some groomers have fake families that seem to be nurturing and well-intentioned. Behind the parent's back, the groomer begins to berate the teen's parents and point out parents' unreasonable expectations, with the goal of driving a wedge in between the teen and his or her parents.

4. **ISOLATE**: This step separates a teen from old friends who share core values. A groomer begins to introduce your teen to "new" friends who are "more fun."

Parents may start to discover that their teen has stopped hanging around old friends, even lifelong best friends. The new friends support and accept the teen, while the old friends disapprove. The teen might begin to lie about activities, saying that he or she is spending time with an old friend when really with the new friend group. Once the trafficker fully takes a teen through this step, the teen is in real and immediate danger.

5. **DESENSITIZE:** This step begins to disorient the teen's moral compass. The groomer starts talking to the teen about having a "better" life, continues to introduce new, older friends, perhaps at a nightclub where the teen somehow gets in, despite being underage. The new friend group fawns over the teen, making him or her feel extra special, reinforcing the idea that the teen's parents are the enemy. The new friends seem to have money and a great lifestyle and entice the teen to begin participating in activities that are normally forbidden (dancing for money, dealing or doing drugs).

6. **CAPITALIZE:** The purpose of this final step is to take a child away from parents through brainwashing, coercion, kidnapping, or a combination of the three. The groomer's intent is to take a daughter or son and make money on him or her. The recruiters wait patiently and take advantage of the right opportunity when it presents itself. They will introduce the teen to a "cool" person, maybe a rapper friend, or DJ at a popular

club in town. Your teen takes a ride with the DJ and after their 18th birthday or goes to a party and disappears, never returning home. In this step, if the recruiters can keep your teen away for more than three weeks, it is very difficult to find and rescue the victim.

Okay parents, take a deep breath. Yes, this information is hard to take in and process, and it is even harder to accept that these dangers are at your son or daughter's fingertips. I commend you for doing the hard work to protect your children from these very real threats.

PROPAGANDA AND HERD MENTALITY

It's strange to include this as an external threat, but considering the last few years, it's clear I must. "Propaganda" in its traditional sense refers to persuasive and forceful communication used to promote political agendas, especially during times of war (think of Hitler). But times have changed, and given the reach and impact of social media and the silos online algorithms create, we now see propaganda as intentional and persuasive communication that targets listeners, impacts their take on positions, and changes their thinking, while getting them to take action on any number of issues without all of the facts—whether on a grand scale (politics, religion, freedoms and liberties, sexual orientation, gender politics, healthcare, the role of law enforcement in society) or more personal and local in nature (the decision of a bullied

CHAPTER EIGHT

student to bring violence into a school or actions a lovesick stalker will take against their interest). We now know this very real phenomenon exists. Coupled with herd mentality, our children can be impacted in thought and ultimately in action and not even know why they are compelled to do something.

Let's add another layer: The internet allows our children to connect with anyone, even "leaders" locally or nationally or across the globe. Kids in today's world think nothing of tweeting, emailing, messaging, or otherwise trying to connect with these people. And sometimes, these leaders reply or have people on their teams reply. It's important to know this as we talk about concepts generally with our kids. Propaganda can be easily spotted. Does an article or piece present one side of an issue and demonize the others? Does it essentially "tell" the reader what to think, or does it present both sides of an issue with the intent of leaving the reader to decide what to think and what position to take? The online world is full of one-sided agendas and so we must help our children to think critically and consider both sides of an issue, not just follow an idea because it appears that "everyone else is doing it." We must teach our kids to be thought leaders, so they are not manipulated by political or marketing agendas.

While we can never avoid or get away from propaganda or herd mentality, the idea here is to make sure your child isn't manipulated emotionally or caught up in others' political or social agendas. The exit strategy is to be a level-headed, independent thinker.

Here are some guidelines to discuss with your child to foster independent thought:

- While "surfing" online, be proactive and mindful of what you allow yourself to consume and who you follow. Ask yourself, do you follow only one party affiliation or one school of thought exclusively, let's say on Twitter or other platforms? Do you allow yourself to hear and explore all sides of a topic?

- How can you research an issue that you believe in, considering a whole spectrum of ideas and opinions? Have you ever reached out to strangers whose opinions you respected to try and engage them in conversation or ask questions? Have they responded?

- How do you form your own true opinion? How do we make sure you don't carry or mirror the emotions of others or engage in herd mentality thinking or mimicry?

- How deeply do you feel about issues? Have you gone too far? Do you have someone you can confide in that is physically in real life known to you and a trusted adult?

- Will you give yourself time to make decisions on issues?

CHAPTER EIGHT

HATE SPEECH

While propaganda has the potential to fundamentally undermine our children, our schools, our community, and societies, hate speech has spurred action resulting in death and destruction—even at the hands of youth who you would never expect to engage in such violence. Hate speech is used to vilify, humiliate, or incite hatred against a person, group, or class of people. It's also actions such as online trolling. It creates a sentiment of us vs. them, or me vs. you coupled with a feeling of true lack of caring for others. Hate speech is a very real issue online right now and our kids come across it daily, whether it be in words, symbols, images, memes, emojis, songs, gaming, digital content, and more. It's important to note, hateful content isn't always obvious. It can be rather subtle and manipulative when ideas are inserted casually, or implied, or issued as just a "matter of fact."

About 64% of U.S. teens have encountered hate speech online.[83] During the height of the Covid pandemic, one organization monitoring online harassment and hate speech found a 70% increase in cyberbullying in just a matter of months, a 40% increase in toxicity on online gaming platforms, a 900% increase in hate speech on Twitter directed toward China and the Chinese, and a 200% increase in traffic to hate sites.[84]

---

83   https://www.ofsms.org/resources/
84   https://www.verywellfamily.com/cyberbullying-increasing-during-global-

DEVELOP AN EXIT STRATEGY

Hate speech was a problem pre-pandemic as well, with more than half of Americans, 53%, saying they were subjected to hateful speech and harassment in 2018.[85] We know this is an issue, especially in the online space. Anonymity, heightened emotions, and the lack of physical factors could mitigate one's actions or words (i.e., your target is not standing in front of you as you attack them) leads to paving the way for a "war of words" (really mean and hurtful words) daily. It's important to help kids compartmentalize what hate speech is and its impact.

We must be careful because of the way a preteen or teenage brain is wired; we know even subtle messages of hate "stick," especially as our kids try to form their identity and values. Kids will often ask me, "What about my right to free speech?" Along those lines, parents often ask if online speech could cause school discipline. These are great questions.

Let's tackle free speech first with a story of a Connecticut woman who was an incoming Government and Public Business Service Analyst working at Deloitte. It was her dream job but she was fired after posting a video that suggested that she would stab people who said, "All lives matter." The Harvard grad took to TikTok where she said:

> "The nerve, the sheer entitled Caucasity to say, 'all lives matter'...Ima stab you. Ima stab you, and while you're

---
pandemic-4845901
85 https://www.usatoday.com/story/news/2019/02/13/study-most-americans-have-been-targeted-hateful-speech-online/2846987002/

CHAPTER EIGHT

struggling and bleeding out, Ima show you my paper cut and say, 'My cut matters, too.'"

The young woman insisted this was a joke and the question then became one of free speech and its protection. So, what do we think? Is this type of threat, okay? Whether real or joke? What does the law say? There is no legal definition of "hate speech," meaning that most hateful language is protected and even legal under the First Amendment of the U.S. Constitution, which guarantees free speech. That said, hate speech crosses the line to become illegal when it directly incites imminent criminal activity or includes specific threats of violence targeted against a person or group. One will argue that the comment above doesn't truly incite imminent criminal activity. But we must remember that free speech applies to our relationship with the government and what charges they can or cannot bring against us. Deloitte, a private company, can choose to demand a certain level of behavior from its employees and terminate those who do not live up to its standard. This ties right into protecting their brand standards—something we now know all about!

Another booming area of concern is with threats students make against their schools.

Look at this example: If a student tweets, "Hey fellow 9th graders, I hate you all. Here's your notice that tomorrow there will be bloodshed at school—I'm done playin'," they can absolutely expect local FBI to show up at their home and make an arrest for a terroristic threat. Adding "just kidding" does nothing. Schools are required to take these threats seriously. A landmark case out of Ohio found that students in public schools do have free speech unless that speech is determined to "materially and substantially interfere" with the operations of the school. This ruling from Tinker v. Des Moines Independent School District (1969)[86] is still the legal standard.

WHAT ABOUT ONLINE SPEECH CREATED BY STUDENTS OUTSIDE OF THE SCHOOL ENVIRONMENT?

Even online speech created outside of school and outside of school hours is subject to disciplinary action when it disrupts other students' rights to feel safe in school and get their education. A ruling out of San Francisco federal court found that off-campus social media created by students and with the intent of disrupting school operations, could be considered "school speech" and be subject to proper school discipline.[87]

So, how do we develop an exit strategy here? While we can't completely avoid the hate speech of others, we can make sure we are not a part of it and we can have plan for when we encounter it happening to others.

1. Talk to your kids about the reality of hate speech.

---

86 https://www.uscourts.gov/educational-resources/educational-activities/facts-and-case-summary-tinker-v-des-moines
87 https://www.uscourts.gov/educational-resources/educational-activities/facts-and-case-summary-tinker-v-des-moines

2. Ask them to define it (language used to demean, insult, threaten, bully, and abuse) and think about what they may have seen or even said lately.

3. If they recognized hate speech, ask them what role they played. Were they a participant, enabler, bystander, or disrupter?

4. Give a clear example: Our children should always disrupt (report) threats against themselves, another person, a group, or the school.

5. How did what was said make *them* feel?

6. How do they think it made *others* feel? Talk through the reality that hate speech is not just demeaning but it has the power to truly impact the target's self-esteem and lead to depression, isolation, anger, antisocial, and self-destructive behavior.

7. Did it change their opinions on people or things?

8. Do they see how the language could have impacted the intended target?

9. Do they understand how online speech, even outside of school hours and off school campus, could be considered part of their school conduct?

10. What are your family values? What moral compass guides them? What is your evergreen rule on hate speech?

11. And most importantly, as they grow and form passionate opinions, how do they manage their feelings, their ideas, and their engagement, in a world with so many different views?

THE UBERIZATION OF DRUGS, PILLS, ALCOHOL, AND MORE

A new reality and one we must take seriously is what I call the "uberization" or home delivery of drugs, pills, vape pens, alcohol, and more. Sadly, while we have no idea this is happening, our kids are viewing drug menus, talking to dealers, and placing delivery orders similar to the way you and I may order a pizza. Who is doing this? Good kids. Everyday kids. Bored kids. Happy kids. Sad kids. Kids who are curious and want to experiment. Kids who have many friends who also do this. Kids who have no idea what they are doing or just how dangerous their actions are.

So, what really happens? It's as simple as one, two, three. Children connect on social media with dealers in a matter of seconds. After looking at a colorful and enticing "menu" of options, they select their drug or pill of choice, and within minutes, can find that item at their families doorstep (parents, remember our rules on apps that have GPS location tracking on—turn it off so connections like these, often made by geographical proximity, can't be made as easily). If they choose not to have it delivered to their house, that's fine

CHAPTER EIGHT

with dealers too. Dealers will meet kids at a nearby park or crossroad. Money is exchanged online or in person. The transaction is easier than you can imagine and cheaper too. At first.

There are so many problems with this—so many. First, before you think, "Well, kids hooked on drugs will do anything" followed by "Thank God I have a good kid," I urge you to go back and reread the opening story of this book—which has impacted me personally to my core. Sammy was a good kid, in one of the best families, with dreams and plans and a path to achieve them all. He wasn't talking to a drug dealer to feed a major drug addiction. He wasn't looking at the colorful drug menu because he necessarily sought it out, or because it was part of his daily and normal routine. He wasn't even looking for drugs. He was a one-time user looking for a prescription pill. And he was targeted. He was curious possibly, bored maybe, or perhaps in pain. Or maybe, just maybe, he ordered it because the dealers and social media companies made it too easy. A click here, a charge of 15 cents there, and—boom—it was delivered. As I said, as easy as one, two, three.

And at the end of the day, Sammy wasn't making a purchase he thought would ever, or could ever take him away from his family and the great life he was living. He purchased what he thought (we believe) was one Percocet pill. Just one pill. But it ended his life almost instantly. How? Because these pills and drugs, pushed by dealers who don't give a damn, are made in labs, or garages or in foreign places with no checks and balances. And sadly, Fentanyl is being used as an additive in a record number of these man-made pills and drugs.

Why Fentanyl? Because it's easy to get, easy to add, and highly addictive if it doesn't kill you. You may have heard of Fentanyl as being a synthetic opioid approved for treating severe pain, such as advanced cancer pain. But illicitly manufactured, Fentanyl is the main driver of recent increases in synthetic opioid deaths. Shockingly, synthetic opioid deaths across the US have increased by 264% from 2012 to 2015[88] and those numbers have shot up even more in recent years. Fifty to a hundred times more potent than morphine, just two milligrams of Fentanyl (two grains of salt) can kill someone upon ingestion. What if you're thinking, My child only smokes marijuana. Well, according to a 2019 study, the most popular illegal drug of choice in 2018 was marijuana with an estimated 43.4 million users in the U.S. alone. That said, dealers know this is a drug of choice so they sell it online and lace it with Fentanyl in the hopes of giving your child a high they'll chase forever. Until it kills them.[89]

As if the problem of uberization of drugs wasn't already a huge issue, add to this the utter lack of control we have over social media tech giants. Section 230[90] of the Communica-

---

[88] https://oudecho.iu.edu/resources/downloads/ECHO%20presenation-%20Current%20Drug%20Trends.pdf
[89] https://oudecho.iu.edu/resources/downloads/ECHO%20presenation-%20Current%20Drug%20Trends.pdf
[90] Section 230 was first passed in 1996 and was intended to enable internet companies to host third-party content and engage in targeted moderation of the worst content without being treated as "publishers," which are generally held

CHAPTER EIGHT

tions Decency Act grants them immunity, plus they have powerful lobbyists and attorneys who ensure their protection above all else, and everyone else. Add to this that when they have determined a dealer is on their site, yes, they close the user's page down, but we know that dealers pop up under a new page almost immediately. Additionally, the social media giants have historically not shared drug dealers' information with grieving parents, nor do they readily hand the seller's information over to law enforcement, under the pretext that it would go against the seller's "right to privacy." So, parents, and kids, please beware. This online jungle that we all need and use and benefit from, also continually presents very dangerous items that can hurt our children and even kill them. The tech giants who have paved the way for these dangerous items to come straight to our doors are under no financial incentive to protect us in the aftermath. Until we all demand that they do.[91]

Given the sheer increase in these cases, many are urging parents to have Narcan nasal spray in the home at all times. Sold over the counter in pharmacies across America, a blast of Narcan in the nose can keep a child alive in the event of

---

accountable for the content that appears in its publication.

[91] Following the traumatic death of Sammy Chapman, his parents, Dr. Laura Berman and Sam Chapman, began fighting for the rights and protection of children, pushing for social media giants like SnapChat and others to allow parent monitoring software like BARK.us to be allowed on their platforms. SnapChat has not allowed any parent monitoring software. To join the movement to change this, please sign the petition #LetParentsProtect on change.org.

Fentanyl poising. Parents, hopefully our kids know exactly what to do if they see drug activity online. It's hard for them and they don't always get it, but we have to keep talking to them until they do. Be proud and loud disrupters. Doing so can protect their lives and the lives of their friends.

IT'S NOT JUST A SOCIAL MEDIA ISSUE

Turns out, just about everything is available on Amazon, psychoactive drugs included. Believe it or not, many goal-oriented kids are purposefully and strategically taking these very dangerous drugs such as LSD, MDMA, psychedelics and psilocybin mushrooms because they believe this will enhance their intelligence or connect them with extra-dimensional spiritual entities. Kids are intrigued by the usage of these drugs brought into the mainstream by public figures and role models such as Graham Hancock, Joe Rogan, and Paul Stamets who speak about their own personal psychedelic experiences often.

Parents beware, our kids believe these drugs are safe because they come from plants and are "harvested and used the same way they were for centuries." The problem is that they are buying them from drug dealers or with a simple "click and add to cart" from Amazon and there is no verification of what is in them. In addition to concerns about Fentanyl finding it's way into just about everything, some kids suffer from hallucinogen persisting perception disorder (HPPD) whereby the psychedelic experience yields

CHAPTER EIGHT

persisting visual hallucinations or permanent alteration of personality. Please have a talk with your kids about these things and ALWAYS check your Amazon account charges.

CYBERBULLYING

I mentioned cyberbullying earlier, but the issue is so pervasive that we need to dig in a little deeper. This is obviously a huge area of concern, and diving in requires us to look at cyberbullying, its effects, the bully, the victim, and possible responses.

Bullying is a repeated, unwanted, aggressive behavior that involves a real or perceived power imbalance, whether in person or online. Historically, bullying involved targeting a person based on race, gender identity, sexual orientation, religion, disability, or body image. Today, bullying is sport; it's a thing kids do to pass time. Their target is picked on a whim and can be a former friend or romantic interest. They can be someone known or chosen based on the momentum of others who also bully. It's reckless. It's relentless. And it's extremely catastrophic for the target.

Cyberbullying is digital bullying. It is done using phones, computers, tablets, gaming consoles, and other tools like text messaging, photos, social media, chat rooms, online gaming platforms, and more to repeatedly target, stalk, mock, copy, and harass others. Many believe cyberbullying is worse than bullying because it's relentless and follows a child home. It is harder for parents to spot and often leaves a child alone,

CYBERBULLYING BY THE NUMBERS

- About 88% of social media-using teens have witnessed other people being mean or cruel on social networking sites.

- Approximately 34% of students report experiencing cyberbullying.[92]

- 73% of students feel they have been bullied in their lifetime, and 44% say it's happened in the last 30 days.[93]

- 60% of teenagers have experienced some sort of cyberbullying.[94]

- 70% of teenagers have reported someone spreading rumors about them online.[95]

- 95% of teenagers are connected to the internet and 85% use social media.[96]

- 59% of U.S. teens experienced cyberbullying or online harassment. 90% say they think this harassment is a problem that affects other people their age. 63% say that

---

[92] https://www.ofsms.org/resources/
[93] https://www.broadbandsearch.net/blog/cyber-bullying-statistics
[94] https://www.pewresearch.org/internet/2018/09/27/a-majority-of-teens-have-experienced-some-form-of-cyberbullying/
[95] https://www.sciencedaily.com/releases/2017/02/170221102036.htm
[96] https://www.pewresearch.org/internet/2018/09/27/a-majority-of-teens-have-experienced-some-form-of-cyberbullying/

it's a major problem.[97]

Why are people cyberbullied?[98]

- 61% for appearance
- 25% for academic achievement/intelligence
- 17% for race
- 15% for sexuality
- 15% for financial status
- 11% for religion
- 20% other

Kids who are cyberbullied truly suffer:

- It affects their existing relationships with others.
- 14% say it negatively impacts their relationship with friends and family.[99]

It affects them emotionally and physically:

- Bullied students are twice as likely as other students to experience headaches and stomach aches.[100]

---

97 https://www.pewresearch.org/internet/2018/09/27/a-majority-of-teens-have-experienced-some-form-of-cyberbullying/
98 https://www.broadbandsearch.net/blog/cyber-bullying-statistics
99 https://nces.ed.gov/pubs2017/2017064.pdf
100 https://pediatrics.aappublications.org/content/132/4/720?sso=1&sso_redirect_cou

It affects them at school:

- 64% say it affects their ability to learn at school and to feel safe at school.[101]

- We know that kids who are cyberbullied are more likely to have trouble adjusting at school.

SELF-HARM FROM CYBERBULLYING

The toll of the emotional and physical ramifications of cyberbullying also leads to mental health and behavior problems.[102] Nineteen percent of bullied students say the bullying negatively impacts how they feel about themselves.[103] How can you tell if your child is being cyberbullied?

Here are some tell-tale signs:

- Shy and withdrawn

- Moody, agitated, anxious, or stressed

- More aggressive toward others

- Protest going out or going to school

- Hide their phones or gadgets

---

nt=1&nfstatus=401&nftoken=00000000-0000-0000-0000-000000000000&nfstatusdescription=ERROR%3A+No+local+token
101 https://cyberbullying.org/new-national-bullying-cyberbullying-data
102 https://www.cdc.gov/violenceprevention/pdf/bullying-factsheet508.pdf
103 https://nces.ed.gov/pubs2017/2017064.pdf

- Irritable when looking at their phones or gadgets
- Skip school
- Stop using their devices all together, coupled with a change in behavior
- Dip in academic performance
- Attempt self-harm or threaten suicide
- Have a new group of friends

HOW CAN YOU TELL IF YOUR CHILD IS THE CYBERBULLY?

While difficult for any parent to admit, shockingly, any one of our kids can be the bully. Not because it's innately in them, but remember, kids are influenced during this stage to do things they wouldn't normally do. It's best to get ahead of it. Take a look at their online and offline behavior.

Do they:

- Stop using the phone or their gadget when someone comes near them?
- Seem more secretive than normal?
- Not hang out or talk to their normal or closest friends?
- Have more of their conversations in secret?
- Spend more time on their devices than normal?
- Seem jumpy or nervous when on their devices?

And side note—it's important to add that adults can be the bullies too. I've seen far too many parents pick on other students they simply don't like.

CYBERBULLYING EXIT STRATEGY

As of 2021, 81% of kids think that bullying is easier to get away with online because nearly 90% of kids who see cyberbullying will ignore it.[104,105] That's a shocking reality and those are sobering statistics. As we go through this book, I am often asking you to ask your child what type of person they will be when faced with these difficult online situations. Again, we are moving them from a million intangible concepts and ideas to a very strategic online way of thinking that covers large areas of content by having them create a plan ahead of time. So, now as it relates to cyberbullying, who will they be? Will they be a participant, an enabler, a bystander, or a disrupter?

I think we agree in saying, let's challenge them all to be disrupters. Please. How can they be disrupters? *Actively*, by calling on the bully to stop. Passively, by sharing good and positive comments about the target, standing with them, and lending a hand to help them through a tough time. They can actively disrupt the bullying by *reporting it* to the social media platforms, to teachers or counselors at schools, and even to

---
104 https://www.cox.com/wcm/en/aboutus/datasheet/takecharge/2009-teen-survey.pdf?campcode=takecharge-research-link_2009-teen-survey_0511
105 https://www.pewresearch.org/internet/Reports/2011/Teens-and-social-media.aspx

CHAPTER EIGHT

law enforcement when necessary. To start, each social media app has a way to report bullying and hate speech. This is a good first step when dealing with harmful content online. When a post or user is reported, the platform might have the post or comment removed, or they may suspend or delete the account depending on the situation. If they choose not to remove the post and/or user, then it's critical that you block the person from reaching you again. When you report a user or account, it is anonymous so the person you are reporting will not know who reported them. Depending on the platform, they might be warned that their profile was reported. Depending on the type of report being made, social media websites can ask you to provide additional information. For example, if another account is pretending to be you, you might be asked to scan a piece of identifying information to confirm your identity.

To Report Content on Facebook:

- Go to the profile you wish to report.
- In the bottom right of their cover photo, click the "..." icon and select Report.
- From there, just follow the on-screen instructions.

To Report Content on Instagram:

- Tap the person's username to open their profile.

- Tap the "…" icon that appears in the top right corner of the screen beside their name.
- In the drop-down menu, tap "Report."
- Select the reason why you're reporting this account and continue with the on-screen instructions.

To Report Content on SnapChat:

- Select the SnapChat icon at the top of the screen.
- Select the cog gear icon.
- Scroll down to "More Information" and select Support.
- In the search bar type "Report."
- In the drop down list, select "Report a safety or Abuse issue."
- Under "What can we help you with?" select "I have a safety concern."
- Choose the type of issue you want to report.

To Report Content on Twitter:

- Go to the profile of the user you wish to report.
- Select the cog gear icon.
- Select "Report" and then choose the type of issue you would want to report.

CHAPTER EIGHT

- You can provide Twitter with more information about the issue you are reporting by selecting "They're being abusive or harmful."
- Twitter will provide you with further recommendations once you've submitted your report.

Now, if your child is the victim of abuse, they need to be able to share what's happening with a parent or a trusted adult. As a family, keep record of every email, text, comment, post, meme, and more. Report it to the school, as well as to the platform, and to local law enforcement if necessary. Create a plan with the school—demand it—that includes the actual steps the school will take to protect your child at school, during all school related activities, walking the hallways, and on the bus. Additionally, connect with a counselor. We need to be giving victims of cyberbullying the tools to climb out from the overwhelming weight of the abuse and move on from it.

Parents: It's also important to brush up on your local laws that pertains to victims of cyberbullying. In Texas, Maurine Molak changed the laws after her precious son David took his life due to relentless bullying. Because of David's Legacy, parents now have many more options when it comes to protecting their kids in school from cyberbullies.[106]

---

106 https://www.davidslegacy.org

RESOURCES:

To talk to someone now:

- Call 1-800-273-8255 (TALK)

For Spanish speakers:

- Call 1-888-628-9454

For deaf/hard of hearing:

- Call 1-800-799-4889

CHAPTER 9

Internal Threats

Nearly 40% of young people report that social media has a negative impact on self-esteem. The other 60% just aren't aware of it.

We've gone through key external threats or forces that influence our kids while online. Now, let's look at what might be brewing *within* them because of time spent in the online world—things they may not even be aware of. This area, while so vast and vague, will be organized in this chapter so you create strategies and plans to get ahead of these internal bombardments. As we go through areas where our kids struggle internally, our exit strategy here is three pronged.

We want each tween/teen to: (1) *Recognize* the issue **(2)** *Intentionally* and *purposefully* deal with it, which includes conversations with you, their parents or caretaker and/or a therapist as needed. But there's one more step: **(3)** Families, after you've gone through these internal threats—I want you to *pull out* the ones listed (or maybe through conversations you've discovered some that are not listed), and decide which ones are areas of concern for you and your kids. I want you to pull out a calendar and do regular, sched-

CHAPTER NINE

uled check-ins focused on those specific issues. And please, stick to those check-ins. There's no sweeping things under the rug here. If we want to enjoy the online world, we must aggressively protect ourselves from the internal damage it can inherently creates. And it's easy to recognize the damage. Nearly 40% of young people report that social media has a negative impact on how they feel about themselves.[107] I would venture to say the other 60% just aren't aware of it.

THE DOPAMINE REWARD LOOP

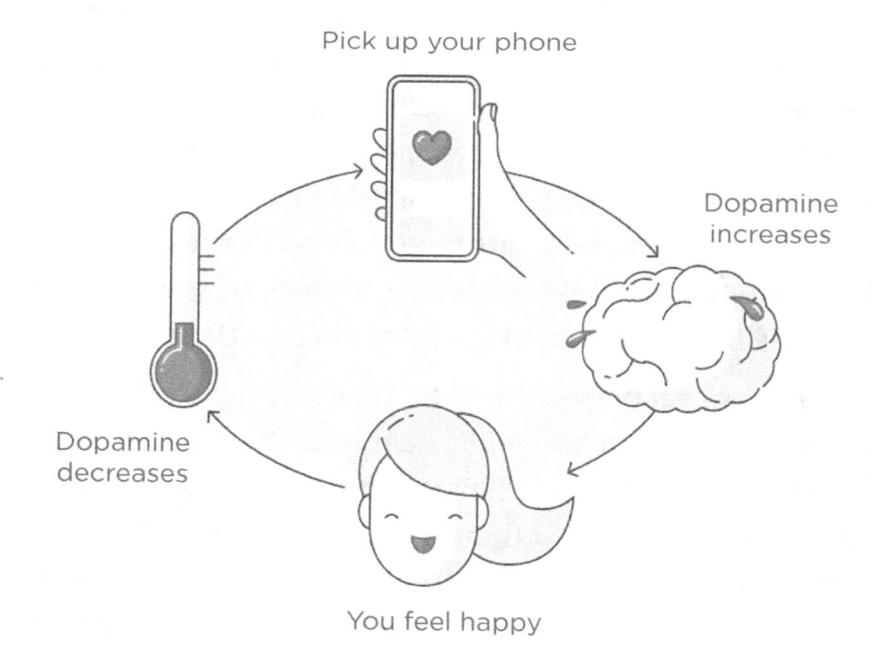

Pick up your phone

Dopamine increases

You feel happy

Dopamine decreases

---

[107] https://www.outbacktreatment.com/the-dangers-of-social-media-for-teens/

INTERNAL THREATS

Exercise 11:
Discuss Internal Threats

Parents, please review the following list of internal threats yourself. Then go back and discuss each one with your child. Ask them if they have struggled in any of these areas.

THE PLAGUE OF COMPARISONS

When young developing minds spend so much time fixated and focused on their peers "perfect" Instagram life, it is easy to see that complexes follow. I'm an adult and I feel the effects of this pressure often. I follow other moms whose feeds indicate that they "have it all together" despite being working moms like me. I see women in my age bracket whose social feeds show them working out or sunbathing in a manner I wouldn't even do at home—alone. It makes me feel "less than," and I study this area for a living. I know the pitfalls. I know everything and anything can be, and is, manipulated through apps and filters. But alas, the effects are there, and feelings do get triggered. Even benign posts can unintentionally trigger a false sense of reality.

One time, our family had just come back from a trip through Europe. My middle daughter took photos—the most beautiful photos I might add, of our time through France and The Netherlands. I shared them regularly in my Instagram stories as we traveled. We returned to friends saying, "What a wonderful trip you just took! The photos! The places!

CHAPTER NINE

How lucky are you!" and in my mind I thought, *For sure, we were lucky to travel, but what the photos did not show was two canceled flights due to plane maintenance issues; having to go through three different cars after dealing with a car accident and a tire issue; being scammed out of $300 near the Eiffel Tower; getting separated from my children in Amsterdam on our last night there; being pulled over by a very aggressive French police officer near the Notre Dame; and so much more.*

It was actually a rather stressful trip, but the photos depicted otherwise. My point is something we all know already; the online world is carefully curated. Even raw moments are often shared with the intent and desire to have emotional impact and build a following. As users we know this, but as consumers, we forget it.

Here's the truth: The online world allows users to place a distorted lens on appearances and reality. It creates deep personal conflicts as we seemingly and constantly find ourselves not living up to what we perceive others have. We are set up continually to judge ourselves against the unrealistic, filtered photos, and manufactured stories of others. Doing this at any age is self-defeating, but for a tween or teen going through physical, psychological, and developmental changes, it's extraordinarily damaging and creates an especially difficult "reality" to navigate.

My generation grew up with magazines that offered a few still-shot, albeit altered, photos of models. We looked at the magazine, dreamed a little dream about looking like those women, and then tossed it aside to get back to our reality. Today, a young adult is constantly measuring themselves against a second-by-second influx of curated content bombarding them via living images, video, and content. And while we all know that apps provide users the ability to airbrush, take inches off, remove pimples and frizzy ends, add teeth whitening and the most perfect filters, we still immediately process photos in a comparative manner where we lose nine times out of ten.

Add to this that our late elementary and middle school-aged kids are going through puberty and working to establish their identities, all at the mercy of a brain not yet developed, while constantly scrutinizing themselves in light of the distorted online realities of others. It's no wonder that online usage has very real effects on our kids. Even the most successful TikTok icons, the ones most kids compare themselves to, deal with this. Addison Rae recently revealed the mental toll of having 70 million TikTok followers has her hyper-fixation on body image. In her interview, she admitted to being in the habit of comparing herself to others, while acknowledging that many do the same with her. She states, "I used to ask myself, *Why doesn't my body look like that? Or why isn't my hair that way? Or why is my face this way?* Or even feature-wise, sometimes I would just really look at myself and pick myself apart for no reason. There is so much going on in the world today, adding self-esteem onto that is really tough. If you can't mentally, emotionally, or physically love who you are, it becomes really difficult to even be happy.

CHAPTER NINE

I know I've not been eating the best during quarantine or maybe not working out as much and watching a lot of TV, but we need to give ourselves grace," she said. "There's this one quote that I love: 'comparison is the thief of joy.' That's so true because when you start comparing yourself to someone, you're just asking to be upset because you're comparing yourself to something that you will never be because you're only you."[108]

Addison Rae really said it best, but beyond what she said, it's what she did—she recognized the issues and she purposefully got herself past the internal complications. It's not a one and done—this takes continual work. However, once you recognize the issue, you really are less likely to be tormented by it. So parents and caretakers, let's have these conversations with our kids often.

SNAPCHAT DYSMORPHIA

Yes, you read that correctly, and it is a thing. Nowadays, kids so desperately want a certain look that makes them fit in that some kids are getting plastic surgery to look like people they are following. Others are actually getting plastic surgery to look like they do when they take filtered selfies. This is shocking. Some kids literally like the way they look via a SnapChat or Instagram filter so much that they are taking those photos to plastic surgeons and willing to have major

---

[108] https://www.yahoo.com/lifestyle/addison-rae-mental-health-body-image-tiktok-201448269.html

surgery to achieve that filtered-photo look. And by filter, we are not talking about smoothing skin out, we are talking about physically changing facial structures.

"SnapChat dysmorphia" is becoming more of a mental illness, classified on the obsessive-compulsive spectrum, yet becoming surprisingly common in millennials and affecting one in every 50 people and growing.[109] These filtered photos have an even greater impact on youth with body dysmorphic disorders because these individuals may more severely internalize the ability to achieve perfect beauty. Plastic surgeons are seeing an increase in patients who want surgery, so they look better in "selfies." A growing number of those patients are sadly under the age of 30. Who would have ever imagined that photo-editing technology would result in a new mental illness?

But we have an exit strategy. Recognize this desire exists and talk to your children about it. Encourage them to intentionally and purposefully seek help when they start having thoughts about going down this road. It's important to catch this early on. If your child finds they like themselves better with filters, or only posting if a filter is present, beware.

THE PSYCHOLOGY OF "LIKES"

Beyond the issue of comparison and physical appearances,

---
[109] https://www.independent.co.uk/life-style/plastic-surgery-cosmetic-SnapChat-teenagers-millennials-dysmorphia-bdd-a8474881.html

CHAPTER NINE

we also must look at the damaging affects the number of likes can have on young minds. Consider this comment from Facebook's founding president, Sean Parker:

> *When Facebook was being developed the objective was: How do we consume as much of your time and conscious attention as possible? It was this mindset that led to the creation of features such as the "like" button that would give users a little dopamine hit to encourage them to upload more content. It's a social-validation feedback loop...exploiting a vulnerability in human psychology.*[110]

Also, consider this: In a normal face-to-face or phone conversation, a person may talk about him/herself roughly 30–40% of the time. On social media, almost all posts are self-centric or tie back to the poster in one way or another. In fact, online, people talk about themselves over 80% of the time. Taking this into account, when you are posting something about yourself and receive a notification of a like or a share, the brain registers that as success. This self-centered behavior is reinforced constantly. And we know this is to be a reality. How many of us post and measure the success of the post on the number of likes? And let's be honest, we don't simply measure the success of the post by the number of likes, we take it as an internal measure of how much we are liked and how successful we are. And then we find ourselves feeling compelled to chase the cycle. *What can I post*

---

110 https://www.outbacktreatment.com/the-dangers-of-social-media-for-teens/

next to keep the momentum going? To get more likes? Our kids certainly think this way with, 40% of children removing privacy settings in order to attract more friends or followers and therefore more likes.[111] Remember what we discussed in Chapter 2—kids are seeking rewards without considering the consequences. This cause-and-effect outcome goes beyond a child's developing brain. It affects all of us so we must understand the power and lure of likes. The scientific consequences here are so undisputed that for a period, Instagram decided to hide likes, making the like counts private.[112] While some applauded Instagram for a move that would make the platform healthier, business partners knew the move would impact the revenue-generating potential of the site so it wasn't executed.

So, what's going on in one's heads with each like? When we post and get a positive response, the brain's reward center releases a bit of dopamine, also known as the feel-good chemical linked to pleasurable activities like food, positive social interaction, and sexual activity. The engineers and designers behind social media platforms purposefully made them this way, modeling the strategy used by the makers of slot machines and techniques to keep users coming back. All of it was done intentionally to tap into the brain's addictive patterns. The app designers knew that when the outcomes

---

111 https://childsafety.losangelescriminallawyer.pro/children-and-grooming-online-predators.html
112 https://www.cbsnews.com/news/instagram-decision-to-make-likes-private-getting-dislikes/

are unpredictable, the user keeps going back until they get a hit or their desired result—be it a slot machine win or a like from a user. It's that drive to create, post, wait for feedback that is never guaranteed, but feels so good once achieved that it keeps users plugged in and coming back for more. When we don't constantly get those "wins" and "likes," this takes a toll on our mental health and wellness. To fix this, we try to post more; we obsess over what we can do differently and how we can engage more and bring praise to our personal pages. The results are a win for social media platforms, but a loss for our kids.

So have your exit strategy. Help your child recognize that most apps are created this way and encourage them to not get pulled into the damaging cycle of "chasing likes." Additionally, touch base with them about this often. Ask them how their posts are making them feel. Ask what the engagement and responses looks like and how this affects them. What aspects of their feelings are healthy vs unhealthy?

FOMO

Add to all of this the reality that kids must navigate FOMO or "fear of missing out." On the one hand, we cannot keep them from online engagement when their entire world is online to engage. On the other hand, as they watch others interact, they may feel a deep desire to take part and not miss anything. This is a reality and one we must understand exists for our children. As an exit strategy, our tweens and teens need to recognize this desire and fear and manage the consequences appropriately.

FAME

In our first tool, we asked our kids why they were really online and what their brand truly was. In doing so, some of us learned a lot about our children by asking questions we've never really asked before. If your child wants to use the online world to become famous or popular, my only goal is that they do this with parents on the same page and a solid strategy in place to keep them safe.

A 2019 survey asked 3,000 kids ages eight to 12 what they wanted to be when they grew up. They were given five professions to choose from: astronaut, musician, professional athlete, teacher, or vlogger/YouTuber. The top choice among kids in the US and the UK was vlogger/YouTuber. Interestingly, the top choice among kids in China was astronaut.[113]

In addition to this painting a picture of the impact the online world has had on children in the US, we need to take this conversation to the next level. The marketplace is responding to this and capitalizing on it. Across the US, on any given weekend, you'll find conferences set up to teach parents and kids about online video posting and the ins and outs of YouTube. Pre-Covid, 75,000 teens spent three days at

---

113 https://www.businessinsider.com/american-kids-youtube-star-astronauts-survey-2019-7

CHAPTER NINE

What do you want to be when you grow up?

Depends on where you are from.

Astronaut is a popular answer to "What do you want to be when you grow up?" in China, but less in the US and UK.

Vlogger/YouTuber is the most popular answer in the US and UK—about three times as likely to be chosen than astronaut.

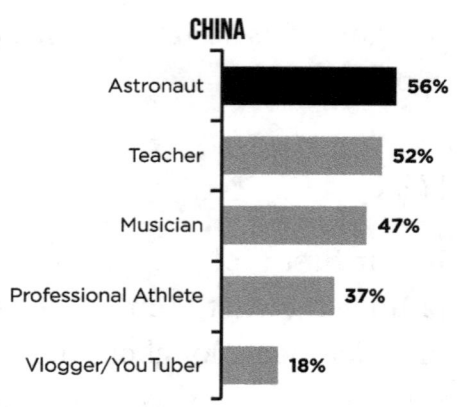

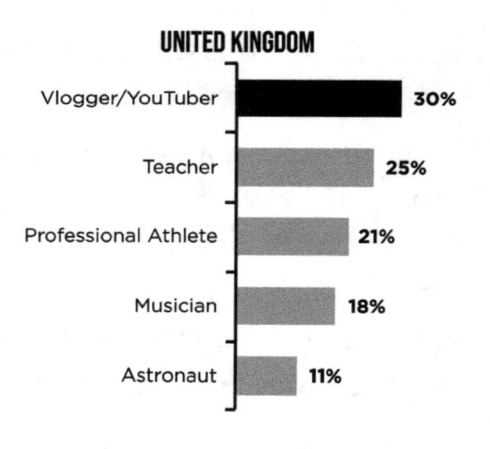

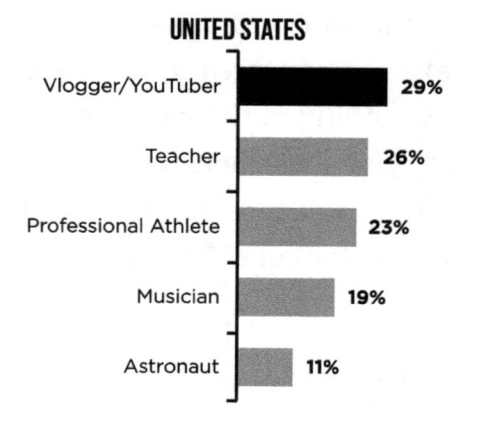

CHINA
- Astronaut: 56%
- Teacher: 52%
- Musician: 47%
- Professional Athlete: 37%
- Vlogger/YouTuber: 18%

UNITED KINGDOM
- Vlogger/YouTuber: 30%
- Teacher: 25%
- Professional Athlete: 21%
- Musician: 18%
- Astronaut: 11%

UNITED STATES
- Vlogger/YouTuber: 29%
- Teacher: 26%
- Professional Athlete: 23%
- Musician: 19%
- Astronaut: 11%

Source: Harris Insights & Analytics LLC.

the VidCon conference just to hear their favorite YouTubers give advice on success.

There are two huge issues that lure children into the "fame" aspect of the online world. One, kids are wired to want accolades and attention. We are addicted to the positive feedback and need it, especially during those shaky developmental years. But here's the second issue: kids, even tweens, know that the more likes, follows, views, and shares you get, the higher the chances are they'll make a financial killing. It's literally incredible to think about. For you and I growing up, there was power in "celebrity" but to become a celebrity, you had to have enormous talent and beauty, study, audition, and still ultimately be "discovered" and move to Hollywood. Today, there is power in influencers, and influencers can be made sitting at home, and even just dancing online in their favorite yoga gear. It seems attainable. These influencers are starting to rule the marketplace. In fact, our kids turn to influencers when it comes to advice on products, brands, trends, and to hear what they think of life's most pressing issues and current events. Influencers to Gen Z (also called Zoomers...did you know that?) and some millennials are almost considered demigods, with nearly 90% of Zoomers saying that they want to become influencers and post content for money.[114]

So, this is an important finding. Even if your child early on indicated that they are not online to become famous, we

---

114 https://morningconsult.com/influencer-report-engaging-gen-z-and-millennials/

CHAPTER NINE

know that an overwhelming 90% of youth on some level want to become influencers and post content for money. There's such a subtle difference here, but it exists. There's fame and then there's online popularity, and the latter might exist even in the heart of the kids who didn't mention fame as an answer in our earlier exercise (but this is why very early on I gave those kids two options: to be "famous" or to "be seen," i.e., popular). Those kids still care about likes, followers, views, and the ability to trend and be influential, and it's something tweens and teens give a lot of weight. I've even seen this in conversations with late elementary-aged children who'll say, "Ben is amazing! He posted a video that got 10,000 views!" or "I love this YouTuber, she has five million subscribers." This is just how today's youth recognize value (sadly).

The financial world is building a future around this new phenomenon. Recent reports show that the buying power of teens is around $44 billion annually.[115] Today's teen does not need cash in their hand or your credit card in their wallet. Instead, they have your card saved to their digital wallet, "add to cart," and make a purchase. It's important to talk to your children about your rules for online spending, which hopefully you did when you developed rules for in-app purchases and online spending.

Because of their buying power, it's also important that kids understand false marketing and scam emails. Adults may be able to see through phishing emails and deceptive

---

115 https://mediakix.com/blog/marketing-to-teens-gen-z-influencers/.

marketing tactics, but our vulnerable kids may not. Depending on your family rules, you may require that your children ask permission before they click on any forms to purchase or give out their personal information. Give them a list of approved sites they can peruse and even "add items to cart" for your approval to purchase. And finally, consider turning off their phone's GPS to prevent them from getting targeted advertisements through text and messaging. GPS tracking, if on, can cause them to get targeted ads you may not want them to have.

Beyond the true desire for kids to become famous, influencers, seen, or popular—and whether that's because they seek fulfillment or seek financial gains—we must take a look at the downside of all of this. To become famous and to trend, kids can be pushed to do things that are truly not in their best interest. The goal of all of this is really to put parents on notice. You've talked to your child, heard their desires, and if in agreement, are working together on a safe plan (that really walks them on the straight and narrow) to build what they are trying to build, with careful strategic thought.

For kids who wish to grow their following in order to sell content, it's important to have an idea of some of the lingo being used around the topic and the potential income.[116]

- A nano-influencer (with typically fewer than 10,000 followers) are starting to get more opportunities and can

---

116 https://www.cnbc.com/make-it/

make a few hundred a post.

- A micro-influencer (with fewer than 50,000 followers on Instagram) can earn almost $500 for a sponsored post.
- After hitting 50,000 followers on Instagram, for example, an influencer could make $1,026 on average for a post.
- With 250,000 followers, earnings jump up to nearly $4,000 per post.

However, everyone must be prepared for when the likes and/or money *do not come pouring in.* Everyone has to be prepared for the criticism that comes from an online community made up of large numbers of people who might be good or really bad. This can be really difficult for children—and for parents. So, what's the exit strategy here? Know that all of this comes with a price and outline of what those things are:

1. What is your child's strategy for building this following?
2. What will you allow or not allow your child to do?
3. How will you both find value? Can your child see this as a project separate from who they are as a person, or does this define them to their core? By the way, I hope it does not.
4. When it starts to get to you or your child, what are the rules? Does everyone have permission to

always be honest and share concerns? Does your child promise to talk to mom or dad or possibly even a therapist as soon as things start to get hard? If this process becomes too consuming or too deflating, is your child willing to step away? *And remember...*

5. In today's world, it's literally the coolest to fight for good causes. Encourage your child to find his or her good cause and weave that message throughout their posting. Align them with a cause, help them to become literal or figurative brand ambassadors – a positive alliance will yield positive impact.

The key to health and safety here is to start truly defining all these gray spaces and create action plans for them, which is exactly what we are doing together in this book!

DEPRESSION

Between the influx of images that are harmful, the cyberbullying, and this already complicated time in a teen's life, the onset of depression is severely on the rise and coincides with social media taking its place in the world.

The impact of social media on tweens and teens was captured perfectly in the documentary *The Social Dilemma*. In it, social psychologist Professor Jonathan Haidt explores the shocking statistics around a "whole generation" of children who have seen a "gigantic increase in depression and anxiety" beginning around the onset of social media, roughly between 2011 and 2013. Eighth graders who spend over 10 hours on social media each week were 56% more likely to report being "unhappy" than those who spend less time on social media.[117] With 13% of 12 to 17-year-olds reporting depression and 32% reporting anxiety, mental illness is huge a concern.[118] It is also a concern for young adults, since 25% of 18 to 25 year-olds report having some form of mental illness.[119] Depression is increasing among girls, with some researchers suggesting that the increase is connected in part to the rise of social media use among adolescents and young adults.[120] Our exit strategy here is no different. We want parents and kids to be aware, know the signs, have conversations, seek help, and set regular check-ins.

Depression is a real consequence of the online world. Parents, I want you to be able to identify the signs in yourself and in your kids. Tweens and teens, I want you to be able to identify the signs in yourself, and guess what? I also want to know if you see this in your friends. Let's ask—who is helping them?

---

117 https://www.center4research.org/social-media-affects-mental-health/
118 U.S. Department of Health & Human Services. Common Mental Health Disorders in Adolescence. Hhs.gov. https://www.hhs.gov/ash/oah/adolescent-development/mental-health/adolescent-mental-health-basics/common-disorders/index.html. Updated May 2019
119 National Institute of Mental Health. Mental Illness. Nimh.nih.gov. https://www.nimh.nih.gov/health/statistics/mental-illness.shtml. Updated February 2019.
120 Twenge JM, Joiner TE, Rogers ML, Martin GN. Increases in depressive symptoms, suicide-related outcomes, and suicide rates among US adolescents after 2010 and links to increased new media screen time. Clinical Psychological Science. 2018; 6(1):3-17.

Signs include:

- Loss of appetite
- Increased risky behavior
- Fatigue, insomnia, lack of concentration
- Loss of interest in activities you used to enjoy
- Socially withdrawn
- Influx of emotional outburst
- Sad language

SUICIDAL IDEATION AND SUICIDE BASED ON SOCIAL MEDIA

We have talked about the amount of time kids spend online throughout this book. This will of course vary with each household. We also know that the more time kids spend online (especially on social media), the greater the chances they will have suicidal ideation. Teens using social media more than five hours daily were 70% more likely to have suicidal thoughts or actions than those who reported one hour of daily use.[121]

It follows that as suicidal ideation increases so would incidents of suicide. And in fact, sadly, we see that as more children aged 10–14 spend more time online, suicide rates

---

121 https://www.ofsms.org/resources/

CHAPTER NINE

have increased by 150%. Along the same lines, incidents of suicide have increased by 70% in older teenage girls compared to rates prior to the launch of social media.[122]

Parents, this is a huge area of concern. We must have an exit strategy in mind, and it starts with knowing that social media and the online world, with all its pushes and pulls, exposures and meanness really hurts our children. Talk to your children about this and ask them if they have ever had suicidal thoughts? If so, why have they had these thoughts? Have you ever started to think of how you would do it? What can we do as a family to help you deal with this? If the answer is yes to any of these questions, seek the guidance of a therapist and have your child immediately get professional help. I will say, plant the seeds early and often. While you are doing a lot of work to ensure that they make the right choices online, there will never be one thing that they do (in public or in secret) that would EVER be worth ending their lives over. Not one thing. Let's say it again and again: **Not. One. Thing.**

SELF-HARM FROM SOCIAL MEDIA

Between cyberbullying, comparisons, chasing likes and the addictive pressures of social media, girls are cutting and hurting themselves at alarming rates. Self-harm by girls 10–14 has increased by 189%–nearly tripling–with alarming rates of kids admitted to the hospital after cutting themselves

---

122 https://www.the-sun.com/news/1487147/social-media-suicides-self-harm-netflix-social-dilemma/

or otherwise self-harming.[123] For girls aged 15 to 19, there has been a 62% increase since 2009.[124] We need to understand this and talk to our kids about why some tweens or teens would ever choose to do this. Through conversations, you can help shape a young child's ability to deal with extreme situations and find other solutions. It's my opinion that often kids self-harm when they have no one to talk to and no way to express their emotion and no strategy to get help. Let's give our kids all these tools from the start and remind them there is nothing they can do or post that would ever warrant hurting themselves. Talk and listen, and when necessary, seek professional help.

ADDICTION

We've talked about the psychology of likes and the addictive nature of online environments. This is impacting all of us. Eighty-one percent of teens in the United States are on social media, and nearly 70% of adults are as well.[125] Beyond the drive to get likes, there are an estimated 210 million people currently suffering from social media and internet addiction.[126]

We're also addicted to the smartphones themselves. While we all yell at our kids to put the phone down, it's almost

---

[123] https://www.the-sun.com/news/1487147/social-media-suicides-self-harm-netflix-social-dilemma/
[124] https://etactics.com/blog/social-media-and-mental-health-statistics
[125] https://www.pewresearch.org/fact-tank/2017/01/12/evolution-of-technology/
[126] https://www.sciencedirect.com/science/article/abs/pii/S0160791X16301634

impossible for them to do so. A recent study found that 94% of participants reported feeling troubled when they didn't have their phone with them (I literally can relate to this) and 80% felt jealous when another person was using their phone. Of those surveyed, 70% literally worried and anticipated feelings of depression and helplessness if their phone was lost.[127]

Another study found 61% of people check their phones within the first five minutes of waking up[128] and that 89% of undergraduate students experience "phantom vibrations," meaning they so badly want to receive a notification that their body and mind start imagining and feeling something that isn't even happening.[129]

Parents and caretakers, if you were to stop and think about this right now, are your children addicted to technology? If so, what? Technology addiction is not just about phones but any electronic that feeds your child's emotions and takes time.

Now it's time to establish clear guidelines and develop an exit strategy:

- Think twice about giving young kids phones and gadgets.

- Limit their screen time (Experts recommend three hours per day tops.)

---

[127] https://www.lemonade.com/blog/psychology-behind-phone-addiction/
[128] https://www.bgr.in/news/61-people-check-their-phones-within-5-minutes-after-waking-up-deloitte-435501/
[129] https://www.sciencedirect.com/science/article/abs/pii/S0747563212000799

- Do not let kids sleep with or wake up to their gadgets or have them alone in their rooms for that matter.

- Remove the gadgets for a period of time. Consider having set times weekly that are designated as "phone free" or "gadget free" for the whole family. This could be one or two evenings a week or one full day a week or on the weekend, for example.

There are many other areas of addiction we must examine that are unique to social media and the online world. These topics are hard to digest, but we must cover them.

PORNOGRAPHY

Pornography addiction is becoming an epidemic among youth in America. Yes, all youth—boys and girls. According to a 2021 analysis of the most visited websites worldwide, two of the top 10 most visited sites were pornographic in nature (coming in at 7th and 9th place). Following Covid, pornography sites received more website traffic in 2020 than Twitter, Instagram, Netflix, Zoom, Pinterest, and LinkedIn, combined. Access to sexual content via video, images, fantasy novels, graphic language, anime, and more is available almost anywhere you go online. The content is so graphic and ever changing that it keeps consumers engaged, even the youngest consumers. Curiosity, plus the physical effect it has on teens and tweens makes them repeatedly go back for more. Early exposure varies with nearly 30% of kids saying their first exposure was "by accident." Nineteen percent were exposed unexpectedly when shown content by someone else, and another 19% searched for it, possibly out of curiosity, but nevertheless intentionally.[130] Another study showed that while 75% of parents believe their children have not been exposed to pornography, 53% of children from those same families had indeed been exposed.[131] Approximately 84.4% of 14 to 18 year-old males and 57% of 14 to 18 year-old females have viewed pornography.[132] We also know that 90% of kids eight to 26 will have seen pornography at some point while online.[133]

The problems pornography present require another book entirely, and while we've touched on this topic throughout the book, I'm going to broad stroke more data for you here:

- First of all, the content is often gruesome, unrealistic, and damaging for young minds forming opinions around sexuality, but kids do not understand this. One recent survey found that over half of boys (53%) and over a third of girls (39%) reported believing that pornography was a realistic depiction of sex.[134] This does not lay a healthy foundation for relationships in adult life.

- The business of pornography is constantly pushing

---

130 https://www.mdx.ac.uk/__data/assets/pdf_file/0021/223266/MDX-NSPCC-OCC-pornography-report.pdf.
131 https://www.bbfc.co.uk/about-classification/research
132 https://www.tandfonline.com/doi/abs/10.1080/10810730.2021.1887840
133 www.guardchild.com
134 https://www.mdx.ac.uk/__data/assets/pdf_file/0021/223266/MDX-NSPCC-OCC-pornography-report.pdf

boundaries, creating more content categories, and tapping into more violence. This affects children with almost half (46.9%) of those surveyed saying their interest in pornographic content grew to enjoy and seek out content they previously found extreme, disinteresting, or even disgusting.[135] Parents, I don't know about you, but I don't want to raise kids who think this way or want this type of sexual experience!

- Children are exploited in the creation of pornography. In 2018, 45 million images of child sexual abuse material (often called "child porn") was reported, according to the National Center for Missing and Exploited Children. In 2019, that number jumped to 69.1 million. And already in 2020, NCMEC's cyber tipline has experienced a 63.31% increase in reports from the same time frame in 2019.[136]

- Additionally, the "teen porn" category has topped porn site searches for the last seven or more years (Pornhub Analytics) with "child porn" becoming one of the fastest-growing online businesses.[137] Those in the industry are abused regularly. It's an avenue to showcase and sell trafficked individuals who become sex slaves. Women are promised fame and fortune and get used and abused instead.

---

[135] https://uclep.be/wp-content/uploads/pdf/Pub/Wery_CHB_2016.pdf
[136] https://www.missingkids.org/blog/2020/Covid-19-and-missing-and-exploited-children
[137] https://www.iwf.org.uk/resources/trends

- Consumption by young adults can lead to pornography addiction, sexual addiction, and erectile dysfunction (in later teen years, especially for boys), the need for medication to reach and maintain normal arousal (also in later years, especially for boys), and an unhealthy understanding of sexual expression, which in the proper context would occur between two consenting adults in a healthy relationship. It all becomes distorted and hinders the ability to have healthy intimate relationships and families as adults.

PORNOGRAPHY USE AMONG TEENS STATISTICS[138]

- 93% of boys and 62% of girls are exposed to internet pornography before the age of 18.
- 70% of boys have spent at least 30 consecutive minutes looking at online porn on at least one occasion.
- 35% of boys have done this on at least ten occasions.
- 83% of boys have seen group sex on the internet.
- 67% of children admit to clearing their internet history to hide their online activity.
- 79% of accidental exposures to internet porn among kids take place in the home.
- 12% of websites on the internet are pornographic—

---

138 http://www.ypacenter.com/youth-pornography-addiction

approximately 25 million websites.

- 2 of the top 100 websites on the internet are porn sites.
- 40 million Americans regularly visit pornographic websites.
- 2.5 billion emails per day are pornographic.
- 25% of search engine requests each day are pornography related—approximately 70 million per day.
- 3% of pornographic websites require age verification.
- The most popular day of the week for viewing pornography is Sunday.
- 10% of pornography users report being addicted.
- The average age a child first sees internet pornography is 11.
- 70% of young men ages 18-24 visit pornographic websites on at least a monthly basis.

I think many of the problems in the online world are tied to this issue. The marketplace is looking for sexual content, photos, songs, dances, videos, acts, and more. So much of the online world seems to be content that is fully pornographic or shades away from it. Parents, this is a difficult conversation to have with kids, and I don't know that you need to share all these statistics with them, but I do want you to know what we are dealing with. I also think that talking to our sons and daughters about the dangers of this industry and the consumption of the products they're pushing is critical. Viewing the content supports the abuse of women in the industry; viewing the content creates an unhealthy view of sexual intimacy; viewing the content literally takes a physical and psychological toll on your body, and signals producers that the marketplace wants more of it. Let's do our best not to view this type of content. Where you think an addiction is brewing, get a mental health professional involved immediately to help your tween or teen or young adult get help.

SLEEP AND HEALTH IMPLICATIONS

A 2018 British study tied social media use to decreased, disrupted, and delayed sleep, which is associated with depression, memory loss, and poor academic performance. Social media use can affect a user's physical health even more directly. Researchers now know the connection between the mind and the gut can turn anxiety and depression into nausea, headaches, muscle tension, and tremors. If your child is having unexplained health issues, this might be the root.

We've already discussed how excessive device use is causing myopia in kids, but the quick-paced effects of the online world have had a huge impact on the attention spans of young consumers, as well. Today it is estimated that the average tween/teen has an attention span of only eight seconds. Just eight seconds. That's about the attention span of a goldfish.

An easy exit strategy here is to limit usage and for sure no longer allow gadgets in the bedroom. Do not let tweens or teens fall asleep or wake up to a gadget and limit use of these items at least one hour or more before bedtime. If sleep disruption continues, see a health professional.

INTERNET GAMING DISORDER/GAMING ADDICTION

If you are a parent struggling with your child's gaming usage, this might help you connect some dots. First, gaming engineers use "persuasive design," which includes built-in elements to keep young minds hooked on certain entertainment technologies.[139] They are intentionally designing addictive platforms. So how do you know when your tween or teen has gone from "loving to play" to being "addicted to playing"? The DSM-5[140] suggests addiction could be an issue when you've been able to identify five or more of the following criteria within a 12-month period.

These criteria include:[141]

1. **Preoccupation with games:** The individual thinks about previous gaming activity or anticipates playing the next game; gaming becomes the dominant activity in daily life.

2. **Withdrawal symptoms when gaming is taken away:** These symptoms are typically described as

---

139 https://medium.com/@richardnfreed/the-tech-industrys-psychological-war-on-kids-c452870464ce
140 The Diagnostic and Statistical Manual of Mental Disease – Fifth Edition
141 https://pediatrics.aappublications.org/content/140/Supplement_2/S81

irritability, anxiety, or sadness.

3. **Tolerance:** The need to spend increasing amounts of time engaged in games.

4. **Unsuccessful attempts** to control or reduce participation in games.

5. **Loss of interest in real**-life relationships, previous hobbies, and other entertainment as a result of (and with the exception of) games.

6. Continued **excessive use of games** despite knowledge of psychosocial problems.

7. **Deceit** of family members, therapists, or others regarding the amount of gaming.

8. **Use of games to escape** or relieve a negative mood (feelings of helplessness, guilt, or anxiety).

9. Jeopardizes or **loses a significant relationship**, job, or educational or career opportunity.

Sadly, many will be able to identify with five or more of the above listed criteria. The situation has gotten so dire, in 2018, the World Health Organization listed Internet Gaming Disorder as an official diagnosis.[142]

---

[142] https://www.who.int/news-room/q-a-detail/addictive-behaviours-gaming-disorder

The impacts of gaming addiction are many:

- The obsession with playing electronic games can be to the point of sleep deprivation, disruption of daily life, and a loosening grip on reality.

- Onset of depression and withdrawal exist when players are not playing.

- One study found that gamers can become risky and unsafe drivers.[143]

- Gamers may not have the tools to deal with the real world (41%) say they play to escape from the real world).[144]

- Gaming addicts might actually have underlying issues, including higher levels of anxiety, aggressive behavior, and neuroticism.

Similar to cell phone and technology addiction, it's critical that we understand what this is, that we name the addiction if it exists in our family, and that we start building tools to exit or deal with the problem. If strategies like the ones listed for cell phone and technology addiction cannot be met, please contact a mental health provider.

---

[143] https://www.nhpr.org/the-exchange/2019-07-15/video-game-design-how-it-impacts-us-and-how-we-study-its-impacts#stream/0
[144] http://www.liebertonline.com/doi/abs/10.1089/cpb.2009.0059

TOOL 3 / SUMMARY

- There are very real threats that come from engaging in the online world—both external and internal.

- External threats come in the form of things our kids will be exposed to online: drugs, pornography, violence, hate speech, etc.

- Internal threats come in the form of things that will brew within our kids based on their time online: depression, self-esteem issues, addiction to technology, self-harm, suicide, obsession with harvesting "likes" etc.

- Parents need to know that if they install blocks, kids can usually get around them. Kids need to understand the threats, buy into their own safety, and have an exit strategy.

- The key is that they "Know the threats, recognize them, and instantly block them."

CHAPTER 10:

Tool 4: Post Like a Celebrity

Celebrity means more than the content itself.
DOMINIQUE SACHSE,
EMMY AWARD-WINNING JOURNALIST & ONLINE INFLUENCER

The fourth and final evergreen tool usually gets raised eyebrows at first. Then, after an explanation, there's an "aha" moment usually followed by, "That's genius!" And it is. So, if your eyebrows are raised at the title of this chapter, stay tuned for a forthcoming "aha" moment.

In my work, I have the pleasure of speaking at schools about important safety issues, particularly as it relates to the online world, of course. When I'm speaking to middle and high school kids (sometimes even late elementary), I do an exercise where I begin by asking, "How many of you are on social media?" Usually, most arms will go up.

"Great!" I reply. They always look at me oddly as they expect that I'll tell them to stay offline.

Next question, "How many of you follow influencers and celebrities you like, love, and admire?"

At this point, every hand that was previously raised goes

CHAPTER TEN

up again.

Then I say, "Even better... Now, I want each and every one of you to post exactly like them."

Silence.

Teachers usually look around the room, as does the school counselor who usually hears the presentation. I love this part because I always absolutely have the attention of these kids.

I go on, "I want each of you to think of your favorite influencer or celebrity right now and go through their posts in your mind. As you go through their posts, I want you to do the following:

- Tell me exactly where they go to school.
- Scour through the posts and write down their home address.
- Tell me the exact town they live in.
- Let's add their office address, license plate number, and a full image of the front of their home."

Silence from the kids. They are now thinking. I continue, "As you do this, I am almost 100% certain that you will not be able to find *any* of that information on their accounts. Why? Because unlike the rest of us, celebrities and influencers have made their safety and protection a number one priority *before* they start posting. They, or their *teams*, have spent hours making sure their personal identifying information is hidden. They or their teams, have spent hours ensuring that the access they give you through their posting never opens the door for you to contact them in real time or in real life. They post—they just do so smartly! I want each of you to *post exactly like they do.*"

They are thinking.

I will usually get this follow-up question: "But [insert reality star name] always shows where she is in real time and films from her home! Sure, we don't know the exact location, but there are tons of pictures! And she shares the town she lives in, and where they are eating right now or where they're going tonight or traveling this weekend!" The kids always make this argument and I love it. They are thinking, and while they are thinking, it is sinking in.

"True." I will say. "But the celebrities, influencers and reality stars who do precisely what you just said also have a team of security following them at all times. They have the ability to ask a restaurant or store to close down to the public if they need to start separating themselves from crowds. They may even have multiple homes to post from, never really giving you access to where they are; these homes are merely a backdrop for the story or image they are painting for their online brand or business. Additionally, given their fame, many are in difficult-to-find neighborhoods with guards and security separate from the security teams they walk around with. Let's start with this simple question: Please raise your hand if you at least have a team of security currently following you at all times."

CHAPTER TEN

Crickets. And sometimes even smiles. They are getting it. These celebrities don't just have the security teams with them at all times, but they also have specialty online teams who do the following to make sure their online followers can never reach them:

- They give their celebrities anonymous phones.
- They purchase phones using an alias.
- They have several different numbers connected to several different untraceable identities.
- They don't register their name with Apple.
- Their teams create private shared encrypted communications (cell numbers, texting, and emails under alias names) to network with close relationships like family and business partners.
- They keep Bluetooth off and do not use iCloud. No GPS tracking is on. (They're not sharing their location in real time on SnapMap!)
- They use multiple levels of password authentication, and so much more.
- They go through the same levels to protect email while they then scour public records to remove names, addresses, emails, phone numbers, and personal information from the internet. Even public tax records are scrubbed.

- They maintain a P.O. Box for all mail, and more.

Smiles and laughs fill the room. They get it. They really get it.

Parents, I know that it's extremely hard—no, impossible—to stay on top of every single thing your child is posting. But if you've talked through their brand, gone through the effects of their post, discussed their community, and educated them on the things that will come their way externally, or brew within them internally, it's time to stop and really focus on posting safely. And *posting like a celebrity* is a great way to do just that. Celebrities and influencers have perfected the art of "safe sharing." Yes, they have teams that are wiping their personal data off public records. Yes, they often are not even using their real names. Yes, they have security teams around them at all times. Yes, they live in gated communities with gated homes. But they still make safe posting a priority. Now, back to our kids. They use their real names online, they do not have anyone scrubbing their personal data off public records, they do not have a security team, nor do they live in double-gated properties. How much more should they make safe posting a priority?

They all need to make it priority number one. And if you share the idea with them in this way, I find that kids get it. It's no longer us being paranoid about an issue they don't think is real. We're now showing them that safe-posting is so important that the celebs and influencers they've been following have been safe-posting all along. It's not about parents being restrictive, it's about giving them the defined purpose and path to post with intention and do it, safely. It's no longer about setting up unrealistic expectations. All of the sudden, it's about understanding their world and using the people they admire most as tools in their tool belt and examples of how to keep safe. And that's a win-win!

POST LIKE A CELEBRITY:

Guidance for kids who decide they want to be seen, build a business brand and public accounts with large communities of unknown people following them: I shared this statistic earlier in the book, but let's revisit it. Two out of ten children between the ages of eight and 11 are aware of safety issues and concerned that strangers may find out information about them.[145] This means that 80% of young children do not even think of this. The percentages are similar for teens and young adults. We have a lot of work to do in this area and it starts right here, right now.

Exercise 12:
Safe Posting Strategy

First, I want you and your child to pick their favorite celebrity or influencer. Visit their social media pages, their YouTube page, and more. Examine what you're able to discover about

---

[145] https://childsafety.losangelescriminallawyer.pro/children-and-grooming-online-predators.html

them. Can you see how they post with safety in mind? Were you able to pull their address or where their company offices are, or their personal schedules? What about their license plate numbers or any other nugget of information that helps you get physically close to them? I bet not. Now, let's arm your kids to do the same.

1. **Always post strategically with safety in mind.**

    - Be extremely mindful of sharing personal information that is identifying. *This is so hard* for kids who usually share without even noticing. Because safety isn't a top priority, a child may very easily share photos in front of their homes (with a home number showing) or photos of them on the field with their school sports team (thereby identifying their town and school). In addition, they may post photos at their day job divulging the location and potentially their work schedule.

2. **Keep private documents private!**

    - Today's teen posts photos of their license plates, report cards, vaccination cards, bad test scores, good test scores, ranking in sports competitions, first check from a new job, an employment review, birth records with an ink-stamped foot ("Look what I just found! How cute!") to parents and grandparents marriage

CHAPTER TEN

license ("Major flashback Friday!") and more. In their desperation for content, they are not thinking about safety, but we need to make safety their top thought. We want them to have all the content they need but to do it all strategically and safely! Talk about these things with them, show them what information predators or bad intentioned people in their vast and wide-reaching online communities can do with personal information they have shared from addresses, towns, banking information, school information, and more. It all creates huge risks for the child and the family.

3. **Don't post photos of your car where your license plate is showing.**

    - It's extremely easy for one of your followers to do a reverse license plate search and find you or your parents' personal information. Hear this another way: I'm not saying don't post with your car, I'm saying cover up the personal identifying information.

4. **Be careful about sharing information on upcoming events or where you are or where you are going in real time.**

    - Typically speaking, online predators work in much more nefarious ways than showing up at a location a child has shared online. That said, when you have a large following and share often, followers begin to consume your content in very personal ways. They may show up just to see you in real life, to take a photo of you (with or without you knowing), or take a selfie with you. What's your plan if the follower makes you uncomfortable? What tactic should your child take If he/she is aggressive or forceful? Remember, most of our children don't have the luxury of security teams, so this leaves our children in a difficult situation to manage alone. Talk it through and have a strategy now, before they post. Some kids have decided to video content of a day of shopping or a restaurant visit and always post a day later to create a buffer in time and space from their online community. A good idea!

5. **Always remember, pictures have time and location stamps and can sometimes work against you.**

    - Most people know that photos taken on today's devices share a person's exact location and an estimated time stamp. A savvy person can go to Google or another search engine to find a photo's exact location. Obviously, this poses a huge safety risk! Additionally, someone really interested can even find out if your photo was cropped and reverse the effects if needed.

6. **Remove GPS location from photos.**

CHAPTER TEN

- It's critical that you remove location data from your photos before you share them. Certain apps advertise that they will remove it for you, but you never know and should never risk it. Can you imagine if anyone who wanted could, right now, take any of the photos your tween or teen has posted and find the exact location embedded in the images? It's terrifying, as this data includes not just location but also things like the exact model of your camera or phone and the date and timestamp of when it was taken. The data (called EXIF data)[146] can even share technical information, including the shutter speed, ISO, and aperture used. Most of us will agree that we do not want anyone to have all this information, so it's imperative that we remove this data when sharing photos.

To hide the location and data on certain photos:

1. Select one or more photos and tap the share button (little square with the arrow pointing up).
2. At the top of the screen, tap the word "Options."
3. Where you see "Include" "All photos data," toggle this off.

To hide the location and data on all photos on an iPhone:

---

146 https://en.wikipedia.org/wiki/Exif

1. Go to "settings" on your iPhone
2. Go to "privacy"
3. Go to "location services"
4. Hit "Never" for photos.

It's important that friends have talked about this as well! What if you child has decided to post safely but is with friends who share photos of them or pull them into live videos exposing where your child is in real time? We need to cover even these potential blind spots. It's easy to do: simply have a conversation with your friends about your intentions to post safely. You can still take photos and do live videos but decide together how you'll do so safely.

Parents, be mindful that sharing too much can also set your child up for identity theft. Ensure your kids are mindful of what they click on and what information they share when taking quizzes and signing up for things!

There are people in your child's online community who may have no interest in accessing your child physically but who are working overtime to get their personal information for financial reasons. Identity thieves love how young adults use social media because they are constantly posting and talking about their best friends, their hometowns, pets, birthdays, favorite sports team and pizza toppings—all of which are usually answers to security questions and passwords. Once they've targeted a young adult online who shares

CHAPTER TEN

frequently and gives a lot of access, thieves sit up, pay attention, and start jotting down information.

So please, talk about this with your kids! Let's make sure our kids are not sharing too many details online—even if they seem innocuous. Over time, it's very damaging. This advice applies to what our kids post on their own platforms but also what they post on other people's platforms. Young adults are the number one targets of scammers because they can steal their identity and no one will ever know until they are getting their first car, or a loan for school. Be careful what apps are downloaded and avoid clickbait! Scammers are constantly sending links and emails, quizzes, and more hoping your kids will click and install malware or start sharing personal information. Kids need to beware!

ADVICE FOR YOUNGER ADULTS WHO LIVE ALONE OR WITH FRIENDS AT SCHOOL

If you are sharing content continually (but are not at the point of having personal security, which I imagine is the case for many of you), I urge you to continue to be extremely strategic in how you post, especially when it comes to being home alone or traveling. You do not want to broadcast to the internet that you are alone, or that no one is home in the house that you've probably shared from on many occasions.

BE MINDFUL OF HOW YOU SHARE YOUR HOME!

It makes me crazy when kids post photos of their front doors or interiors that both showcase their homes and what all the internal locking mechanisms look like. I know this sounds paranoid, but to someone following your child online who may potentially become obsessed, these photos are a gift. Please, I'm not saying don't post from outside or inside the house, but I am saying post strategically and with safety in mind. Don't show house numbers or landmark identifiers. Be smart!

THOUGHTS ABOUT POSTING WHILE TRAVELING

To post or not to post while traveling...this is always the hardest question. Traditionally, safety experts say not to share when you are traveling or won't be home. They also advise that you only share photos of a trip after you have returned. I have mixed feelings about this. Their guidance is based on a concern for the safety of your home, but my feeling is, if you've been taking a safety-minded approach all along and have been protecting the location of your home, I am less of a worrier about this issue. I also know that crime trends across this country are changing with "would be" thieves caring less about targeting a home when families travel and more about targeting a home they know is a good hit. Talk with your family about it and make a judgment call that works best for you. **And a quick side note:** As a public safety advocate, let me remind you that when you do travel, please make sure your home alarm company (if you have one!) is able to reach you while you are out of the country. I've talked to many people whose alarm companies were directed to call their office. That does you no good when you are traveling!

AND ONE MORE TIME - GPS LOCATION AND SOCIAL MEDIA APPS.

I've mentioned this several times: GPS tracking really creates a huge vulnerability. It's a good idea to turn location off of all social media apps when you are using them. Here's how:

To turn off the location on social media apps on an iPhone:

1. Go to "settings" on your iPhone.
2. Go to "privacy."
3. Go to "location services."
4. Hit "Never" for the apps you want to hide your location while using.

To turn off all location services including GPS on an Android phone:

1. From any Home screen, tap Apps.
2. Tap Settings.
3. Tap Privacy and safety.

4. Tap Location.

5. Side the Location Switch left to the OFF position. This disables all location services, including GPS.

PARENT HACK: You can keep digging on your iPhone.

1. In the same page where you are choosing never to share your location while on certain apps, hit "system services" at the bottom.

2. Then go to "Significant locations" (You'll need to enter the child's phone password or facial recognition to get into this part of the phone).

3. "Significant locations" allows your iPhone and iCloud-connected devices to learn places significant to you in order to provide useful location-related information in Maps, Calendars, Photos, and more. Significant Locations are end-to-end encrypted and cannot be read by Apple. This is an important area to look at, even to check every once and a while on a child's phone. Parents can discover a lot by doing this.

CHAPTER TEN

PHISHING, HACKING, AND MALWARE

I cannot stress the importance of making kids aware of these harmful tactics to manipulate their vulnerable minds. Our children need to know that scammers are super active on technology. They will send fake emails that look like they are coming from schools, modeling agencies, casting directors, your email provider, Amazon, or a number of big companies trying to get a young adult to click and fill in information. With every click, you run the risk of malware being installed on your systems, and with any information shared, you run a huge risk of identity theft taking place.

Additionally, kids must be mindful of what type of content and photos they store on their computers and phones. There are countless stories of kids who have been hacked and had very personal videos or content shared with the world without permission. It's a terrible thing to experience. Yes, kids should be free to have private content on their private devices, but at the same time, if we are connecting with the online world in a constant manner, we have to be prepared to deal with the realities of that world, and sometimes hacking does take place.

Beyond hacking, here's where we urge kids *not* to share user passwords with even best friends, romantic interests, or anyone else but parents. Kids go into each other's phones all the time and look through photos, texts, notes, emails, and more. With a quick screenshot and share, personal information can be taken quickly. Also remember, if you are out and about, don't leave your phone unattended. Others can pick it up and start going through it as well.

DO YOU STILL NEED TO POST LIKE A CELEBRITY IF YOU HAVE A PRIVATE ACCOUNT?

Yes. The reality is, even a child who has a private profile is posting on platforms where things live forever and are somehow always searchable and eventually sharable. Whatever you post can always end up in the wrong hands and create vulnerabilities for you. So, parents and kids, guard your safety, proactively and continuously. You'll never regret doing so.

Other safeguards for all kids:

- **Know how to report and block:** When it comes to safety, all kids need to know how to report and block harmful people. Go over each account with your child and make sure you, and they, know how to do this.

- **Get passwords:** Parents, *always* have all usernames and passwords for your child's phones, iPads, computers, and other gadgets.

- **Set preferences:** Whether your accounts are set to private or you have a public profile, take time to set up preferences within social media apps and sites.

- **Delete, delete, delete!** Use the features within each environment to delete problematic comments, wall posts, pictures, videos, notes, and tags.

- **Don't feel obligated to respond:** Your child should not feel obligated to respond to messages or friend/follower requests that are annoying or unwanted. They should feel comfortable to disallow certain people from communicating with them or reading certain pieces of content you share. A reminder here to turn off location sharing and think long and hard before using the "check-in" feature.

- **Keep personal conversations private:** I know this is really hard, but try not to communicate with a best friend or two over an entire social network that many are following and watching.

- **Secure your profile:** Kids must be smart about passwords and share them with parents only! Not friends. Avoid using obvious answers for security or recovery questions. Try not to access your online profiles from public devices (library computer or at the Apple store!) Be sure to have the latest malware and antivirus software installed on devices and make sure all accounts are set up with two-factor authentication.

TALKING TO YOUNGER KIDS

When talking to younger kids, those soon-to-be exposed to the online world for the first time, here's a good way to go about *all* of this above:

1. Ask your tween or teen to help you set up your

profile. Click on privacy settings together and make sure kids get why this is important.

2. Talk about passwords and profile photos.

3. Go onto social media and start looking up friends and people they know in real life. Show them how much information is already there.

4. Talk through public vs. private accounts.

TOOL 4 / SUMMARY

- Teaching kids to post like a celebrity means being thoughtful, smart, and strategic about the way they post and share.

- It's imperative that they understand how to protect all of their personal information, including photos, chats, texts, videos, emails, and more.

- They need to be smart about passwords to protect themselves from identity theft and manage GPS and tracking scrupulously.

- **Parents:** We need to remind kids not to overshare or use social networking sites as a place to fill a void, feel popular, and hook up with other users. The internet is 'public domain' and they do not have the privacy or anonymity they think they do.

- Please, remind kids that everything posted is kept–even if an app claims the content disappears. Nothing is ever truly gone.

CHAPTER 11

Resources for Parents

Parenting in the digital age is not for the faint at heart.

Congratulations on making it to the last chapter of this book. It's a lot of information, I get it. If your head is spinning and you are feeling completely overwhelmed, pause and take a deep breath. On page 281 is a checklist that will help serve as a guide as you go back through the exercises in this book. This chapter also includes a quick reference to terms, online slang, emojis, info on safety software, and more.

I said at the start, parenting in the digital age is not for the faint of heart. I wish I could just snap my fingers and tell you that if you do all of these things that everything will be ok for your family. I can't guarantee it. But I can tell you that by taking responsibility, you are setting a powerful example that will impact your kid for the rest of their life, even if there may be pushback today. You are communicating to them they are valuable to you, which is what every child wants most in the world—to know they are loved and important to their parents. Having confidence in your love will empower them to make better decisions online and create a foundation of confidence and wisdom for the future.

CHAPTER ELEVEN

I think the hardest part for us as parents is watching our kids grow up and knowing when to trust them and knowing when to trust that we've done enough to prepare them for the great big world ahead. We do have to remember that kids are resilient. We may not be able to protect them from every hurt, but we can teach them how to heal, and grow, and learn from life. That is the opportunity you have with this book.

Now, while I lay out the foundation and tools to proactively keep all of our kids safe online, and especially in an ever-changing online world, I also promise that those of us in the field will keep studying platforms, gaming consoles, and online chat rooms. We will keep advocating for change, for new and stronger safety parameters. We will keep getting even more tactical in fighting for legislation and education that puts the safety of our children above all else.

To that end, we can't do it alone. I, along with all the organizations fighting for your kids, need your help. We need your support. We need you to use your voice. But most importantly, your child needs you to use your voice.

I want to invite you to connect with me online to get the most up-to-date safety information and tools I'm working on personally; and also to explore ways you can make a difference with your voice—by taking action. And if you can, consider financially supporting some of the amazing nonprofits on the frontline of the fight for our kids, such as, Crime Stoppers. Together we can make a difference today and for future generations.

RESOURCES FOR PARENTS

rania.mankarious.1

theraniareport

@theraniareport

CHAPTER ELEVEN

Step by Step Action Guide for Parents

FOUNDATIONS:

- [ ] Where will your child be online? Review platform "buckets" on page 93 and determine family rules of engagement for each permitted type of app (Exercise #1 page 101).

- [ ] Discuss challenges and chain letters with your kids (Exercise #2 page 106).

- [ ] Review pages 86 and 105, tips for talking to teens.

TOOL 1: DEFINE YOUR CHILD'S BRAND

- [ ] Discuss Tool 1 with your child. Go through Family Brand Discussion (Exercise #3 page 132)

- [ ] Discuss the Brand Development Starter Questions (Exercise #4 page 138) and "Start with Why." Review the chapter and examples.

- [ ] Discuss the brand-building basics and brand refinement (Exercise #5 page 147)

RESOURCES FOR PARENTS

- ☐ Discuss the importance of exclusivity and not giving full access of oneself to all (page 148).

- ☐ Discuss a code of ethics and aligning with family values.

- ☐ Do the self-search (Exercise #6 page 150)

TOOL 2: DEFINE YOUR CHILD'S COMMUNITY

- ☐ Discuss with your child the three types of community members: known, acquaintance, unknown (page 159).

- ☐ Discuss all types of people who might be connected or following your child (page 161).

- ☐ Discuss the Evergreen Red Flags (Exercise #7 page 165)

- ☐ Talk to your child about all the accounts they have. Let them know that you know about fake accounts. Review each account and do the assessment of your child's community. Delete and block any suspicious followers (Exercise #8 page 169).

TOOL 3: DEVELOP AN EXIT STRATEGY: KNOW, RECOGNIZE, AND BLOCK

- [ ] Discuss the 3 roles in an encounter on page 180.

- [ ] Review the key external threats. Has your child encountered these? (Exercise #9 page 183)

- [ ] Review the 6 Steps Process of Human Traffickers and signs of grooming (Exercise #10 page 200).

- [ ] Review internal threats (Exercise 11 page 229).

TOOL 4: POST LIKE A CELEBRITY

- [ ] Review my opening story (page 259)

- [ ] Do the celebrity search exercise and develop a Safe posting strategy (Exercise #12 page 264).

- [ ] Remove GPS location and time stamps from photos (page 267).

- [ ] Discuss posting safety with friends or anyone who posts about you.

- [ ] Review dangers of identity theft (page 269).

OTHER SAFEGUARDS

- [ ] Review how to block people on each app with your child.

- [ ] Make sure you have all passwords to your child's devices and accounts.

- [ ] Set preferences for the device and each app.

- [ ] Remove GPS location from social media apps.

- [ ] Set usage rules: How much time will they be allowed online? What are the "no tech" hours? Where do phones go at night?

- [ ] Review Online Absolutes and Posting Guidance on page 286.

CHAPTER ELEVEN

SAFETY SOFTWARE

Parents, don't hesitate to use software to support you in your endeavors to help you keep your kids safe. I personally prefer BARK.us. Bark helps families manage and protect their children's online lives. This software monitors 30+ of the most popular apps and social media platforms, including text messaging and email, for signs of digital dangers. Their screen time management and web filtering tools help parents set healthy limits around how and when your kids use devices and alerts parents when things seem questionable or dangerous. To learn more about BARK go to www.bark.us.

ONLINE ABSOLUTES

Absolutely Never Do

- *Never* film a fight. *Please.* Never film it, and never share it. Report it immediately and get help for the victim, immediately.

- *Never* film a sexual encounter. Never film it, and never share it. *Report it.*

- *Never* take a sexual photo of yourself and share it with another. Never.

- *Never* encourage cyberbullying, cyberstalking, or suicidal ideation and never like or share posts that do so. Report it. Intervene for the sole purpose of getting people help.

- *Never* film, live stream, share, like, or comment on anything that engages in civil or criminal liability. *Remember, bullying, fights, sexual content, vandalism, animal abuse, drinking, drugs, some online challenges, and more can all fall under this category.*
- *Never* share passwords, addresses, phone number, or other personal information online.
- *Never* share sensitive information attached to a court case.
- *Never* meet someone in person who you "talk to" (notice I didn't say "know") online.
- *Never* get in a car with someone you only know from your online engagements.
- *Never* take a pill from someone who sold it to you online. This includes smoking marijuana and using a vape pen.
- *Never* text and drive. Fourteen percent of fatal crashes involve the use of a cell phone. Additionally, research has found that dialing a phone number while driving increases your teen's risk of crashing by six times, and texting while driving increases the risk by 23 times. (NHTSA)

CHAPTER ELEVEN

POSTING GUIDANCE AND IDEAS FOR KIDS

While the online world can teach your kids a lot of things, there are some things it just can't. Some things, like character and values, have to be instilled at home. I think this list sums it up pretty well:

> *10 Lessons I Want To Instill In My Kids*
> *If you're thankful, show it.*
> *If you love someone, tell them.*
> *If you're wrong, fess up.*
> *If you're confused, ask questions.*
> *If you learn something, teach others.*
> *If you're stuck, ask for help.*
> *If you made a mistake, apologize.*
> *If you trip, get back up.*
> *If someone needs help, help them.*
> *If you see wrong, take a stance.*
>
> @7_secrets_of_relationships

To that end, here is a list of the types things your kid can do online everyday:

- Find a contact you know who is celebrating a birthday and share a birthday greeting.
- Share a positive story, either one you find, or one you

create yourself.

- Highlight a cause you believe in and in a positive way, share information on it to educate others.
- Share your good eating habits.
- Share a workout routine.
- Find a few friends to post compliments about online.
- Tag people who inspire you.
- Look for artists whose work makes you laugh and share their posts.
- Share a GoFundMe account (make sure it's legit first though!).
- Encourage the success of a friend who has already shared they are about to take a major test or whose team is facing an important game or who is about to perform (Remember! Only do this if your friend is already sharing that they have this going on).
- Share a talent you have online, provided that it fits into your brand.
- Share five things you are thankful for and challenge others to do the same.
- Share old photos of grandparents or parents that are funny or sentimental.
- Share posts that advocate tolerance, acceptance, inclu-

sion, and anti-bullying sentiments.

- Share posts that talk about courage, kindness, or hope.
- Share polls. Ask people if they prefer "this" or "that."
- Ask people what they are passionate about in an IG Questions post, for example .
- Ask people what their dreams are in an IG Questions post, for example.
- Put the phone down from time to time and schedule in-person time with people in your life. You can even post, "Shutting down while I spend real time with my bestie."
- Be a role model and leader.
- Show kindness to animals via videos of loving on your pet or grooming him/her at home.
- Cheer on those who need it.

IT'S OKAY TO SAY "NO"

Recently on *The Balanced Voice* podcast, I interviewed Chris McKenna, founder of Protect Young Eyes, who produced the popular documentaries, *The Social Dilemma* and *Childhood 2.0*. He made the statement, "The biggest lie we tell ourselves is that children must be online." And while my strategies in this book are designed to help keep kids safe while they are online, I completely agree with him. The following was posted online and sums it ups:

> *I find myself worrying most*
> *that when we hand our children devices,*
> *we steal their boredom from them.*
> *As a result we are raising a generation of*
> *writers who will never start writing,*
> *artists who will never start doodling,*
> *chef's who will never make a mess in the kitchen,*
> *athletes who will never kick a ball against the wall,*
> *musicians who will never pick up their aunt's guitar*
> *and start strumming.*

–Author unknown

Parents, if you find that your kid is falling into addiction or cannot handle the pressures of the online world, it's ok to say "no." It's okay to take breaks. It's okay to let them get bored and explore the offline world. In fact, it's more than okay. It's encouraged.

CHAPTER ELEVEN

Quick Reference Section

**Definitions of important terms,
some discussed in this book.**

- Section 230 of the Communications Decency Act—Title 47 of the United States Code enacted as part of the United States Communications Decency Act, that generally provides immunity for website platforms with respect to third-party content. It specifically states: **"No provider or user of an interactive computer service shall be treated as the publisher or speaker of any information provided by another information content provider"** (47 U.S.C. § 230).

- **True acquaintances:** Someone you are familiar with, see in real life, but do not know (think the person at the grocery store - you see them often but do not know them).

- **False acquaintances:** Someone you literally do not know but are connected to online. They may feel like an acquaintance because you share a social media connection or are directly connected but if that is your only connection to that person, they are not an acquaintance

- **Brand:** Identifying practices or information that defines who you are or what something is.

- **Bystander:** This person sees what is going on but stays quiet or neutral. They neither participate, nor enable, nor stop the activity from taking place. In their silence, they allow the negative activity to continue.

- **Catfishing:** A process where a fictional person or fake identity is created on a social networking device with the goal of targeting a specific victim. The deceptive activity is usually used for financial gain or to compromise the victim target in some way, to intentionally upset them or harm them.

- **Clickbait:** An online headline or thumbnail link designed to attract attention and entice users to follow, read, view, or listen to the linked piece of online content. Content is usually purposefully deceptive, sensationalized, or otherwise misleading. Clickbait can be used for a range of purposes including to get advertiser views or help ill-intended creators to install malware.

- **Cyberbullying:** The use of electronic communication to bully a person, typically by sending messages of an intimidating or threatening nature.

- **Cyberstalking:** The repeated use of electronic communications to harass or frighten someone, for example by sending threatening emails

- **Digital Footprint:** The data left behind your online use. Digital Footprints can be passive and active. An active digital footprint is when the user has deliberately shared information about themselves on social media or websites. Passive footprints are put together based on what

CHAPTER ELEVEN

companies have collected from your online use.

- **Disrupter:** This person takes action to break the cycle of bad behavior. They do not share, like, or positively engage. Instead, they block, report, and thwart negative or dangerous behavior.

- **Dopamine:** Also known as the "feel-good" hormone, is neurotransmitter that is released when your brain is expecting a reward. When you begin to associate certain activities with pleasure, the anticipation can be enough to raise dopamine levels. This can apply to using your phone to check messages or social media posts to food, sex, shopping, drugs and more.

- **Egirl or Eboy (also known as e-kids):** A species of "emo" that's become a youth subculture with a specific look and usually found on TikTok, Tumblr, VSCO or online gaming platforms. Videos by e-girls and e-boys tend to be flirtatious and many times, overtly sexual. They have been seen to sell nudes, "thirst traps" or even time with themselves.

- **Enabler:** This person sees what is happening and actively allows it to continue. They do not block, they do not report, they do not encourage the activity to stop; but rather, they pave the way for it to grow by liking another persons' post.

- **EXIF data (Exchangeable Image Format):** Descriptive data (meta-data) is an image file that includes the date the photo was taken, the resolution used, the shutter speed used, the focal length and additional camera settings.

- **Geotags:** The process of appending geographic coordinates to media based on the location of a mobile device. Geotags can be applied to photos, videos, websites, text messages, and QR codes, and could also include time stamps or other contextual information.

- **Hidden Apps (also called Vault Apps):** Used on cell phones to hide things like photos, files and even other apps. Usually used when user (child) wants to hide content from someone (parent or guardian). Many hidden or vault apps look completely harmless and are often overlooked.

- **Human trafficking:** Modern-day slavery involving the use of force, fraud, or coercion to obtain some type of labor or commercial sex act.

- **Macro-influencers:** Less than a million followers

- **Micro-influencer:** Less than 50,000 followers

- **Nano-influencer:** Less than 10,000 followers

- **Orbit:** Describes men who lurk on a young girl or woman's social media account in the hopes of eventually connecting with her to have sex with her.

- **Participant:** This refers to someone who is actively engaging in online activity. They post, like, comment or share.

- **Persuasive Technology:** This refers to the idea that digital tools like smartphones, and apps for gaming and social media, for example, alter human thoughts and behaviors by intentional design.

- **Phishing:** A type of social engineering where an attacker sends a fraudulent message designed to trick the victim or target into revealing sensitive information to the attacker. Attacker could be trying to steal personal information or get inappropriate photos. Attacker could also be trying to deploy malicious software on the victim's infrastructure like ransomware.

- **Pre-Frontal Cortex:** A part of the brain located at the front of the frontal lobe. It is implicated in a variety of complex behaviors, including planning and greatly contributes to personality development including personality expression, decision making, and moderating social behavior.

- **Ransomware:** Malware designed to encrypt files on a device, rendering any files and the systems that rely on unusable. Attacker then demand ransom (i.e., money) in exchange for decryption and the release of the target's files/system.

- **Sharenting:** Over sharing by a parent whereby their child's photo and interests, sometimes school, grade and teachers, likes and dislikes are shared over social media.

RESOURCES FOR PARENTS

- **Sexting:** The sharing of sexually explicit images, videos or messages via an electronic means.

- **Sextortion:** A form of sexual exploitation where the offender uses coercion and threats to compel the victim to produce sexual images or videos engaging in sexual acts. In some cases, the offender already possesses nude or sexual images of the victim, and is threatening to release them if the victim will not do as the offender commands.

- **Smishing:** The fraudulent practice of sending text messages purporting to be from reputable companies in order to induce individuals to reveal personal information, such as passwords or credit card numbers.

- **Stranger:** Someone you literally do not know; someone truly unknown to you online and in real life.

- **Thirst trap:** A sexy photo posted on social media to attract attention. It can also refer to a person who you consider to be sexy, as in a social-media "crush."

CHAPTER ELEVEN

Emoji Dictionary

From https://www.drugaddictionnow.com/2018/10/03/emojis-give-youth-a-new-way-to-communicate-about-substance-abuse/

👌👅 = penis

✋ = vagina

🍑 = butt

💨 = vagina

🕯️ = you're being ghosted

🐍🐌 = coy, especially in a relationship

💻 = ejaculation

🔺 = oral sex or sexual activity

😦 = frisky

🌶️ = spicy, inappropriate content

🔯✡️ = mean spirited in tone

🍀 = marijuana / weed

🙊 = sexual activity

🍒 = breasts or testicles or virginity

🐻 = involving nudes

👝 = yes, agreed

🏠 = sexual activity

🐼🔺🐼 = it is what it is

298

RESOURCES FOR PARENTS

❄️ = Crystal meth

🍭🥤⚪💊 = cough syrup of mixing the prescription medication with Sprite soda and Jolly Rancher candies

💨 = vaping

💎❄️🎮👅 = methamphetamine

😴💤🐎🎵 = heroin

💎🔑❄️🐍👃🎮⚪ = cocaine

🐴 = used to ask how high the drug potency is

⛽ = used to indicated a person is gassed or high or drunk

☕❤️💊👤⚪ = MDMA usually sold in pill form

✈️ = refers to a drug dealer

For more information on current and changing emoji meanings, go to www.bark.us.

CHAPTER ELEVEN

Slang Terms

Source: *Text Slang Decoded* https://www.bark.us/blog/teen-text-speak-codes-every-parent-should-know/

AF
As f**k

A mood
A relatable feeling or situation (often shortened to the single word, "mood")

And I oop
Used when something is really surprising or provocative

And that's on [something]
Used to indicate that you've just shared a truth that needs no further discussion

ASL
Age/sex/location

Bae
Significant other or crush

Basic
Someone who is viewed as boring or a conforming person

Bet
A response indicating agreement.
Example: "Wanna go to the store?" "Bet."

RESOURCES FOR PARENTS

Bih
Short form of b*tch

Body count
The number of people someone has slept with

Bruh
"Bro," can be used to address anybody

BTS
A Korean boy band popular with tweens and teens

Bussin'
Awesome. Example: These tacos are bussin'.

Cappin'
Lying

CEO of [something]
To be a representative of some activity or thing. Example: "Taylor is the CEO of sleeping in late."

Cheugy
Used to describe someone or something that is basic, out of date, or trying too hard

Cursed
Used to describe something (usually an online image) that is unsettling or creepy

Cringe
Causing feelings of embarrassment or awkwardness

Daddy
An attractive man, usually older, who conveys a sense

of power and dominance

Ded
Used when something is really funny or embarrassing. Example: OMG that meme has me ded!

Dope
A way to describe something as cool or awesome

DTF
Down to f*ck

Egirl/Eboy
A young person with emo-inspired, punk-rock style

Facts
An emphatic way to acknowledge the truth of someone's statement

Fam
Friends

FBOI
F**k boy; a guy just looking for sex

FINSTA
Fake Instagram account

FOMO
Fear of missing out

Fire
Amazing

FWB
Friends with benefits

Gas
Can refer to marijuana, be used to describe something that's cool, or be used as a verb to mean "hype someone up"

Ghosted
Ending a relationship by completely disappearing with no further communication

Goals
Something you want or aspire to

GOAT
Greatest of all time

GTG
Got to go

Gucci
Something good or cool

Hentai
Graphic anime pornography

High key
1. Very interested in 2. Actively spreading information

Hits different
When something is better than it normally is because of different circumstances. Example: "A cold soda just hits different when it's super hot outside."

CHAPTER ELEVEN

ISO
In search of

IYKYK
"If you know you know"; meant to imply that there's an inside joke

Juul
Type of e-cigarette that is small and discreet; 'pods' are used for smoking

Karen
Used to refer to an entitled mom

KMS
Kill myself

KYS
Kill yourself

Lit/Turnt/Turnt Up
Something that's active or popular, can also refer to being stoned or drunk

LMAO
Laughing my ass off

(L)MIRL
(Let's) meet in real life

LMP
1. A term that means "like my pic" or
2. Sometimes stands for "lick my p***y"

RESOURCES FOR PARENTS

LOL
Laugh out loud

Low key
1. Somewhat interested in 2. Keeping information secret

Meal
Someone who looks good enough to eat.
See also: "Snack" or "snacc"

Netflix and chill
Getting together and hooking up

No cap
Used to indicate that someone is not lying

NP
No problem

OFC
Short for "of course"

OK, Boomer
Calling out an idea that is outdated or resistant to change

OMFG
Oh my f**king god

PAW or PRW
Parents are watching

PIR
Parents in room

CHAPTER ELEVEN

Plug
Term used to refer to someone who can "connect" you with drugs; a drug dealer.

PMOYS
Acronym that stands for "put me on your SnapChat"

POS
Parent over shoulder

P911
Parent emergency

ROTFLMAO
Rolling on the floor laughing my ass off

Salty
To be bitter or cranky about something

Same
"I can relate"

Shading
Where teens gossip about another party without naming them; also "throw shade" means to talk about someone

Ship
Short for "relationship"; also used as a verb to indicate a desire to see two people together. Example: I ship Taylor and Jamie.

Sis
Short for "sister" but can be used to address anybody; usually used to express that drama has occurred

RESOURCES FOR PARENTS

Skeet
To ejaculate

Smash
Means to have casual sex

SMDH
Shaking my damn head

SMH
"Shaking my head," meaning "I don't believe it" or "that's so dumb"

Snack
Describes an attractive person

Snap Streak
Created when friends send snaps every day, creating a streak

Snatched
On point, very good, or well styled

Spam
A fake social media account

Squad
Close friend group

Stan
A teen slang term meaning an overzealous or obsessive fan of a particular celebrity

STFU
Short for "shut the f**k up," can be used as an

expression of disbelief or to cyberbully

Swoop
To be picked up in an automobile

TBH
To be honest

Tea
Gossip or interesting news shared between friends

Thicc
Having an attractive, curvy body

TF
The f**k, as in "who TF you think you are?"

Thirsty
Desperate for attention, usually sexual attention

Thot
Stands for "that ho over there" and is often used instead of "slut"

Trash
"Terrible," "unacceptable"

Turnt
Excited and having a good time, often with the help of drugs or alcohol

V
"Very"

Vibing
Chilling out, having a good time, or identifying with a certain kind of energy

VSCO girl
A style characterized by Hydro Flasks, Crocs, and scrunchies

WAP
Wet ass p*ssy

Woke
Socially or politically conscious

WTF
What the f**k?

WYA
Where you at?

WYD
What you doing?

YAAS
A very emphatic yes

YEET
1. A very strong word for yes. 2. To throw something.

Zaddy
A well-dressed, attractive man of any age

CHAPTER ELEVEN

Less Frequently Used Teen Slang Terms

420
Marijuana reference

11:11
Popular time to make a wish

ASB
As balls. Example: I'm high asb.

Chad
A hyper-sexual young man

Chill
Relaxed or laid back

Coney
Slang for "penis"

CY
"Cover your ass" or "see ya"

Dabbing
Refers to concentrated doses of cannabis; also a dance craze

Dongle
Slang for "penis"

HEAF
An acronym for "High Expectations Asian Father"

RESOURCES FOR PARENTS

Hulk
A 2mg generic benzodiazepine bar, which is green

ILY
I love you

IRL
In real life

JK
Just kidding

OKURRR
Variation of "OKAY" made popular by rapper Cardi B who defines it as something that is said to affirm when someone is being put in their place

School Bus
A 2mg Xanax bar, which is yellow

SH
Sh** happens

SUFF
An acronym meaning "Shut up, f**k face"

Spam
A fake social media account

TDTM
Talk dirty to me

WUF
Where you from?

CHAPTER ELEVEN

Index

A

Addiction 247, 255

Addison Rae 231, 232

Alcohol 60, 74, 104, 162, 199, 201, 211, 308

Apps 13, 24, 33, 43, 48, 84, 91, 92, 93, 94, 95, 96, 97, 99, 100, 101, 102, 103, 104, 105, 106, 113, 114, 116, 151, 164, 170, 196, 211, 229, 231, 236, 268, 270, 272, 273, 275, 285, 286, 295, 296

B

Blackmail 189

Block 188, 284

Brain development 54, 55, 58, 60, 62, 69

C

Catfishing 293

Chain letters 5, 91, 106, 107, 312

Challenges 11, 59, 84, 91, 106, 107, 108, 109, 110, 111, 116, 143, 146, 166, 282, 287

Charli D'Amelio 170

Child exploitation 192

Chrissy Teigen 128, 130

Community 153, 158, 165, 166, 169, 193, 283

Community Red Flags 193

Cyberbullying 96, 216, 217, 219, 221, 293

Cyberstalking 186, 187, 293

D

Depression 243, 244

Drugs 32, 33, 35, 49, 60, 74, 104, 162, 164, 199, 200, 201, 202, 211, 212, 213, 215, 258, 287, 294, 306, 308

F

Fame 135, 237, 312

Fentanyl 31, 32, 212, 213, 214, 215

FOMO 236, 302

G

Gaming 17, 23, 24, 35, 37, 62, 63, 64, 65, 66, 67, 68, 84, 86, 97, 103, 113, 182, 183, 184, 185, 187, 193, 195, 206, 216, 255, 256, 257, 280, 294, 296

GPS Tracking 103

H

Hacking 274

Hallucinogen persisting perception disorder 215

Harassment 186

Hate speech 206, 313

Hidden apps 99, 295

I

Influencers 239

Internet gaming disorder (IGD) 255, 256

J
John Clark 199, 200

M
Malware 107, 270, 274, 276, 293

Myopia 77

Myths 22, 38, 39, 69

N
Narcan nasal spray 33, 214

P
Parent hack 114, 273

Phishing 274, 296

Pills 32, 164, 211, 212, 213

Pornography 79, 98, 249, 252

Predators 48, 80, 162, 167, 168, 192, 197

Propaganda 95, 203, 204, 206

Psychology of "Likes" 233

Puberty 54, 57, 58, 60, 231

R
Rania's Golden Rule 90

Report 188, 222, 223, 224, 286

S
Self-harm 219, 246

Sexting 73, 79, 80, 81, 297

Sextortion 189, 192, 297

Sleep 254

SnapChat dysmorphia 232

Suicide 245

U
Uberization of Drugs 211

V
Violence 42, 63, 189

Violence in media 62